DEATH IN THE GREAT SMOKY MOUNTAINS

Death in the Great Smoky Mountains

Stories of Accidents and Foolhardiness in the Most Popular Park

Michael Bradley

Guilford, Connecticut

An imprint of Rowman & Littlefield

Distributed by NATIONAL BOOK NETWORK

British Library Cataloging in Publication Information Available

Library of Congress Cataloging-in-Publication Data is available on file.

ISBN 978-1-4930-2375-2
ISBN 978-1-4930-2563-3 (e-book)

∞™ The paper used in this publication meets the minimum requirements of American National Standard for Information Sciences—Permanence of Paper for Printed Library Materials, ANSI/NISO Z39.48-1992.

CONTENTS

INTRODUCTION

THE GREAT SMOKY MOUNTAINS NATIONAL PARK STRADDLES
the state lines of Tennessee and North Carolina and is within
a day's drive of about half the population of the United States.
Not surprisingly, it is the most visited of all the national
parks, with up to ten million people a year coming to enjoy
the attractions of the area. Most of these visitors use only
two roads: the Trans-Mountain Road between Cherokee,
North Carolina, and Gatlinburg, Tennessee, and the Little
River Road, which leads from the Sugarlands Visitors Center near Gatlinburg to Townsend with a branch leading to
Cades Cove. Such crowds of people sometimes threaten to
overwhelm the more popular roadside attractions, but visitors willing to leave their cars behind for a few minutes, or a
few hours, can find the solitude of wilderness and wildness.

Covering more than eight hundred square miles with
elevations ranging from about 875 feet above sea level to
more than 6,643 feet, the park is very diverse in its climate.
By driving from Gatlinburg on the Tennessee side of the
park to Cherokee on the North Carolina side, one passes
through as many climate zones as if one had driven from
Tennessee to Quebec. The Canadian junco has no need to
migrate from Tennessee or North Carolina to Canada for the

summer; it simply needs to fly from the borders of the park to the mountain crest in the middle. Parts of the Tennessee and North Carolina zones are typical of the southern region of the United States, yet Newfound Gap and Clingmans Dome, along the high crest between the two often called "State Line Ridge," are like Canada. With this great diversity of climate and habitat, the park is home to an astounding variety of flora and fauna. Over seventeen thousand species of plants and animals live in the park, and scientists estimate there may be from two to three times as many more as yet unidentified.

The Great Smokies also contains a unique collection of buildings that give a look into the Appalachian lifestyle of the nineteenth century, a way of life once followed all along the frontier of the United States. At Oconaluftee Visitors Center there is a collection of nineteenth-century buildings that have been moved from various locations, many of them from within the park, which recreates a typical mountain farm. At Cades Cove other buildings are scattered along the road that loops through the cove, with a focal point being Cable's Mill, a working mill utilizing water power to grind corn into meal. Cabins can be found along Airport Road in Gatlinburg as it enters the park on its way to becoming the Roaring Fork Motor Nature Trail. Walking along park trails that once were roads, one may suddenly come upon cemeteries, reminders that people lived and died in the mountains long before the area became a park, as happens in the Cataloochee area.

There is no admission fee to enter the park. Congress authorized the creation of the park in 1926, but no money was appropriated for land acquisition or development. The states of Tennessee and North Carolina provided some money, and land was purchased from timber companies. The Rockefeller family donated five million dollars to assist the undertaking and schoolchildren participated in fund drives, giving pennies and nickels for the cause. It was not until 1934 that the park was considered to be established, and even then it took six more years to build the hiking trails and other facilities to welcome visitors. When President Franklin Roosevelt came to dedicate the park in September 1940, he reminded those assembled for the ceremonies that the legislation establishing the park had declared it to be "a pleasuring ground free to the people." This was considered only proper when so many private citizens had helped to create the Great Smoky Mountains National Park.

The National Park Service (NPS), a division of the Department of the Interior, employs the people who care for the park and its visitors. These folks are usually called "park rangers," and most visitors, on seeing these people wearing their distinctive green and gray uniforms with the distinctive "Smokey Bear" hats, do not realize what a wide variety of skills and tasks these rangers undertake. (By the way, Smokey Bear is properly associated with the US Forest Service, not the NPS.) Some of the NPS personnel you will meet in any park are seasonal rangers, employed for the busiest seasons in a particular park, and often moving from park to park in search of a succession of these seasonal jobs. Some of the rangers are law enforcement rangers, trained and authorized to act as law enforcement officers under the authority of the US government, since all national parks are federal property. This category of rangers is responsible for public safety and other issues concerning protection of the park and its visitors. Many rangers are involved in interpretation of the park, which includes leading guided walks, doing programs at campgrounds and visitor centers, manning the visitor centers, and generally representing the park to the public. Maintenance employees are not rangers but have the task of keeping the park clean and repairing or building facilities in the park. However, these Park Service employees may be the first to hear of an emergency in the park because they make the rounds of the campgrounds and picnic areas on a regular basis. There are some rangers park visitors probably will not meet. These are the administrators who work with the park budget, handle purchases for the park, and do many other necessary but out-of-sight jobs. Also generally out of sight are the resource management rangers, scientists and historians responsible for protecting the natural and historic resources of the park. All these people are ready and willing to help make a visit to the park a pleasant and safe experience. Some of them are called on to risk their lives in doing this; park rangers meet a wide variety of people who are visiting the park, and some of those people cause trouble or get into trouble. Park rangers share the same dangers as do special agents of the FBI, the Secret Service, and the agents of the Bureau of Alcohol, Tobacco, Firearms, and Explosives. A ranger may work in a beautiful place, but the job is demanding and sometimes dangerous.

Consider, with so much to offer, is it any wonder that the Great Smoky Mountains is the most visited of all the national parks? But even beauty can have a harsh side. Ten million visitors annually can, and do, create traffic problems that sometimes lead to accidents, even fatal ones. People who go hiking without proper equipment, especially without sturdy shoes, turn ankles or injure their feet.

On August 10, 2015, rangers responded to a call for help from Joey Watson, a twenty-year-old college student who was hiking the Miry Ridge Trail, which connects the Jakes Creek Trail with the Appalachian Trail. Park Service personnel trained as paramedics hiked for several hours to reach Joey and, on arriving, found he had broken his ankle. It was estimated it would take twelve hours to bring the injured hiker out of the park if he were carried, so the Tennessee Highway Patrol—the only state agency equipped to handle air evacuation rescues—was contacted to bring in their hoist-equipped U-1 Huey helicopter. This effort and expense was caused by Joey simply slipping and falling while walking on an established trail, the sort of accident that could have happened on a city sidewalk. Those who decide to leave the trails and go bushwhacking may find they have bitten off more than they can chew when the terrain becomes rougher and the foliage denser than they anticipated.

When animals are encountered they may look cute, but they are wild animals; in the case of bears, the more they become accustomed to people the more dangerous they become, for they lose their fear of humans and begin to look on them as the source of handouts in the form of potato chips or fried chicken. There are few up-close encounters with bears even so, and every effort should be taken to make sure one does not occur.

Each year up to one hundred people get lost in the park, and this can happen suddenly. Most of these cases are resolved in a few minutes and almost all end in a happy reunion with families. For example, in 2000, a six-year-old boy from Florida wandered away from his family at Clingmans Dome, one of the most frequently visited places in the park. Three days later he was found quite safe sitting beside a stream, eating berries. Some cases do end in tragedy.

Park rangers train for search and rescue missions and, in carrying them out, they sometimes risk their own lives. Whether the end of a search is happy or tragic, it costs money. A short search of two or three days may cost twenty-five thousand to fifty thousand dollars; a longer search will cost hundred of thousands of dollars. People on the ground, searching trails, have to be housed and fed; helicopters to search from the air or to transport search teams to remote locations are very expensive. Each national park budgets some money for search and rescue missions, but once the cost is more than five hundred dollars per searcher per day, the regional office of the Park Service helps with the cost. In very expensive cases there is a contingency fund that can be used to help pay for the mission.

Total costs for search and rescue in the Great Smoky Mountains National Park in 2011 were $133,068 for 108 incidents, five of which included fatalities. Costs for 2012 reached $253,550 for 104 incidents, which included two fatalities. The 2012 costs included the search for Derek Leuking and Michael Giovanni Cocchini (see chapter 6). There are about one hundred search and rescue missions a year with most of them being carry-outs for people with broken legs, blown knees, broken ankles, and heart problems. Beyond this, most of the other searches extend over two days. When hiking in groups a single hiker or a couple will sometimes wander off, and it will take a little while for them to reconnect with their group; sometimes people will take one trail up Mount LeConte and, inadvertently, come back down a different trail so they are at a parking spot miles from where they left their car.

Waterfalls are the most common sites for rescues. Despite warning signs people will climb on the slippery rocks, and they fall. Of the one hundred calls annually for rescue missions some fifty to sixty are for people injured at Abrams Falls, Laurel Falls, Rainbow Falls, and Grotto Falls. Rivers also call for a number of rescues each year, especially along the Little River near Elkmont, at the Sinks, and at the area known as the "Wye" where the Little River Road forks toward Cades Cove in one direction and Townsend in the other. Park rangers do not rescue only people. Dogs are not allowed on most trails in the park, but occasionally a pet gets into trouble in an area where they are allowed. Rangers have been lowered into sinkholes to rescue stranded animals.

Obviously, the park cannot predict how much money will be needed for search and rescue in any given year. The lack of an entrance fee to the park is a mixed blessing. People can enter the park as often as they like and incur no expense, and many local people visit a dozen or more times each year; on the other hand, the park is denied a large sum of money in missed fees. This makes the budget for the park very tight with little room for extra expenses. With ten million visitors annually, there is wear and tear that requires maintenance by the Park Service. Keeping the restrooms at picnic grounds clean, keeping the two main roads in good order, and providing visitor centers where people can become oriented to the park and get answers to questions is costly enough, but visitors who get in trouble cause the park extra expense. The Friends of the Great Smoky Mountains National Park, a private group made up of people who love the park and whose membership is open to all, have helped with the cost of rescues. In 2008 the Friends of the Park donated money to help purchase a one hundred thousand dollar vehicle that serves as a command post for rescue operations. The vehicle carries ropes and pulleys, medical equipment, swift water rescue equipment, as well as food and water.

Given the cost and trouble a search and rescue operation places on the park and its personnel, one would think the rangers might be ready to criticize those visitors who get into trouble. Instead, most rangers are caring and understanding. Rangers know the Great Smoky Mountains offer physical challenges that are easy to underestimate, so even an experienced hiker can take on more of a challenge than they are prepared to meet or can become disoriented.

What is the likelihood that a person may need to be rescued or that a death will occur during their visit? Many inexperienced visitors express concerns about bears or snakes. Sometimes someone says they are afraid because they do not know who may live in the hills. In the history of the park there has never been a recorded death caused by a snake bite, and only one death has been the result of a bear attack. The people who live in the hills are among the most hospitable, helpful, and kind-hearted people to be found anywhere on Earth. Most deaths in the park are from auto accidents, caused by impatient people trying to drive above the usual 30 mile per hour speed limit posted on crooked roads that often have no guardrails. The park roads were built to allow visitors to enjoy the beauty of the park, not to speed from point to point, and guardrails are often absent so as to allow an unhindered view of the scenery. The second most frequent cause of death is drowning. This may sound odd since the park is a mountain setting, but the sparkling streams can be deceptive. Rain several miles away can cause a sudden rise in the water level, slick rocks on the bottom of the stream provide treacherous footing, hidden obstructions can cause stumbles, and powerful currents can sweep people away. Water sports are not recommended in the park; but at the end of a long, sweaty hike the cool water looks so good! A wade in the water can be fun and safe, but plunging into a pool can be very dangerous, as many have found. Climbing up a waterfall, with its slick, mossy rocks, can lead to a fatal fall.

The park is a very safe place overall. There are few accidents, much less fatalities, given the large number of visitors. Common sense and adherence to the simple Park Service rules keep most visitors as safe as they would be at home.

However, ignoring common sense and reasonable rules can quickly get a person in trouble. The mountains are wilderness, and wild animals are truly wild. The terrain of the park is rugged. Slopes are frequently steep, so much so that a hiker who goes off a developed trail may find the ground staring him in the face as he prepares to take his next step; the ascent may be almost vertical. In addition, the Smokies get a lot of rain, up to eighty-five inches a year in some parts of the park. This means the vegetation is thick and tangled. One hundred species of trees grow in the park, and about 95 percent of the park is covered in forest. In areas called "laurel hells," the mountain laurel or rhododendron may be so thick that a person cannot penetrate it; the prevalent plant called "dog hobble" adds to the challenge of going cross-country. Streams are swift and their bottoms are often slick, so that wading in them or across them can lead to unexpected plunges into the cold water, albeit these streams are marked by lovely cascades and spectacular waterfalls. The park rangers do all they can to keep visitors safe, but it is up to each visitor to follow the simple rules posted in frequently visited places or which common sense suggests. With a little care a visit to the Great Smoky Mountains National Park is a pleasure; being careless can be fatal.

Some of the people in the following stories failed to follow the rules, some had bad luck, and some paid the ultimate price for their actions. Some of the people who did not follow the rules were lucky and came out alive. Some people knew the rules, followed them, and survived an experience that might otherwise have caused their death.

When you visit the Great Smoky Mountains National Park, please remember that the most dangerous animal in the park is you—or a human being like you.

CHAPTER 1

Death Before There Was a Park: Jasper Mellinger

A MAN HAD TO WORK LONG AND HARD TO MAKE A LIVING for himself and his family in the Smokies. Jasper Mellinger knew that for a fact. That was why he was undertaking the long, steep path that led from the Elkmont area of Tennessee to the Hazel Creek community on the North Carolina side of the mountains. Jasper was a blacksmith as well as a farmer, and his skills as a smith were always in demand, especially in areas where logging or mining were going on. As a blacksmith Jasper could repair tools, forge hooks for dragging logs out of the woods, repair simple machines by making new parts, and act as a farrier, putting shoes on horses, mules, or oxen. Once the crop of corn in his fields was mature enough to require no additional cultivation, a window of time was open for Jasper to seek extra work.

Jasper had known hard work all his life. He had been born on a farm in Auglaize County, Ohio, in 1837. His father had died when he was eleven years old, leaving a widow and four children: Jasper, Colin, Florence, and Lenora. His father had just sold some land to a neighbor, and court records show he died before a deed was executed, leaving the family with little money and forcing the family to scatter. It is not known what happened to the rest of the family, but Jasper moved to the Smoky Mountains. There he met Martha Varnell, who was nine years younger than he, and they were married. This move likely took place following the Civil War because their first child, Lenora, was born to the couple in 1872. A son, Charles, was born in 1874, and another son, Edward, followed in 1877. The Mellingers were not a large family, but a lot of work was required just to live, especially since the family owned only about thirty acres of land, not all of which was fit to farm. Their home, a simple two-room cabin and an adjacent barn to shelter livestock, was located near Roaring Fork Creek, today just outside Gatlinburg.

By 1901 Jasper had only himself and Martha to support. At age sixty-four he had lived a full life, by the standards of the day, but he was still considered a strong man and he still worked hard. The farm produced vegetables that Martha preserved, and corn to make meal for bread and to provide feed for the pigs and cows they owned. Cash income came from Jasper's trade, although much of the pay he received was in the form of barter—vegetables, meat, etc.—with his customers. Jasper also owned a rifle, and he usually carried it with him wherever he went just in case he had a chance of a shot at game for the pot.

In 1901 Jasper decided to go "over the mountains" to the Hazel Creek area in North Carolina. Several small communities were scattered about the hills there because there were deposits of zinc, iron, and copper. Just a few years after Jasper took his final trip toward the area, a man arrived in the Hazel Creek area who would make the mountains and himself famous. Horace Kephart. But in 1901 the Hazel Creek area was known for logging and mining. At first it had been hoped that gold would be found there, but the shiny ore proved to be copper. At first the price of copper was so low it was not economically feasible to develop the deposits, but at the beginning of the twentieth century the price of copper had risen. Now there were several small copper mines in the area and one of them usually had work for a blacksmith. Jasper took his rifle, his pocket watch, and a little money, told his wife he would be back as soon as he could, and set off walking.

From his home along Roaring Fork Creek, he headed toward the Elkmont community instead of following the Cherokee road. The road, really a rough trace, led up to the backbone of the Smokies, crossed the spine at Road Gap, and then went on toward the town of Cherokee in North Carolina. By going to Elkmont Jasper could cross the high peaks by trails he knew well, not have to achieve so much elevation, and be on a more direct route for Hazel Creek once he entered North Carolina.

Shortly after crossing a spur of Sugarlands Mountain, Jasper picked up the headwaters of streams that led into the Elkmont section. Although he was not many miles from Roaring Fork, the difficulties of travel meant not many people were to be met along the way.

After walking several miles Jasper reached the Ownby farm. The Ownbys were a large family with many in-laws and relatives in the Elkmont area, and the house of the patriarch always welcomed guests who brought a fresh face to the table and, perhaps, fresh news to the ears of the family.

Allowing travelers to spend the night was a well-established part of the tradition of hospitality in the mountains. Jasper spent the night with his hospitable hosts, enjoying the hearty food put on the table, and then repaid them by sharing all the latest news and gossip from his neck of the woods. The work day in the mountains began at daylight, so the group did not linger long around the fire that night but soon "hit the hay," or, more probably, got into a bed with a feather-stuffed mattress. Even a guest likely had to share a bed with a member of the family of the same sex.

One member of the family who remembered Jasper's visit was Lemon, called "Lem," Ownby. He would live until 1984 and would be the last leaseholder living in the park (some individuals who refused to sell their land to the park were given lifetime leases). After a hearty breakfast Jasper thanked the Ownby family and then turned his face toward the main ridge of the Smokies. Even for a strong man accustomed to hard work, the route he had chosen to follow would be a challenge. Jasper may well have followed Jakes Creek, passed through Jakes Gap, then picked up the lead above Panther Creek, heading toward Lynn Prong with the goal of Cold Springs Knob. From that point his route would be toward the upper reaches of Hazel Creek.

As one looks at the mountains, it is obvious there are gulches leading up their slopes. These are often the beds of streams of drainage systems that rise high on the mountains. These, however, do not make the best route to follow on foot. The streams have cut deeply into the surface of the mountains, sheer rock faces ten to thirty feet high frequently block the way as the stream tumbles over waterfalls or cascades, and the moisture from the stream encourages the growth of tangled masses of rhododendron and mountain laurel. The best walking is usually found along the ridges, or "leads," which separate the stream valleys. So Jasper set off, following a stream until the slope began to grow too steep and the vegetation too dense, then he took to the ridges.

From a distance the mountains seem to rise in an unbroken ascent to the ridgeline of the high crest, which appears level—but this is deceptive. The mountains are formed of a succession of ridges, so a walker goes up a ridge, then down some, then back up again. Even the crest of the mountains is a succession of ups and downs. The descents are not as great as the ascents so the traveler is gaining altitude at all times, but from the crest of one ridge to its bottom, one will lose some of the hard-won altitude and will then have to gain it back. Jasper was accustomed to such travel and made steady time, although his pace was steady rather than rapid and he stopped to drink at springs and stream crossings.

Back at Jasper's home in the Roaring Fork area everything was serene. Martha went about her usual household chores: feeding chickens and pigs, milking cows, preparing food for the evening meal. Jasper was expected to be away for several days and there was no expectation that anyone would come to their cabin to tell her he had arrived in Hazel Creek. The daily routine of life continued for several days. No doubt Martha and her oldest son, Edward, talked over the matter from time to time, but still Jasper was not seen or heard from. Then Martha began to wonder when Jasper would return. Every time she heard their dog bark or heard a distant voice she expected to see him coming back up the track to their cabin. Wonder changed to worry, worry changed to fright, fright slowly gave way to grief. Jasper had disappeared. But when and where and how? Sympathetic travelers carried messages from her to the Hazel Creek area, but when replies finally came back there was no news of her husband. Martha became convinced that Jasper had never arrived at his destination. But hope still flickered.

Two and a half years after Jasper was last seen, Baus and Stuart Ownby, members of the family with whom Jasper had spent the night, went on a hunt up onto the high ridge of the Smokies. They followed game trails, scouted the grassy peaks or balds to see if game was present, and they took a look at pools of water where deer or bear were likely to come for a drink. As they looked for footprints along the banks of one pool, they made an unsettling discovery: human bones! Then they found more items, including a rifle with the initials J M carved into the stock. Jasper Mellinger? Then they found a pocket watch and some money.

Mother Nature likes to keep things clean. In a wilderness area the body of an animal or of a person may lie undisturbed for a time, but it then becomes food for animals, birds, and insects. In the Smokies, bears are the first to claim a body since they are the largest animal, but bobcats and possums also feed on carrion. Crows and buzzards are notorious for being scavengers, and, whatever is left, insects finish off the task. Nothing is wasted in the natural process and a body may be reduced to scattered bare bones in a matter of days.

The local sheriff was called and an officer was sent to the scene. Because so much time had passed, no clues were to be found as to how the person had died, but suspicions grew that the remains of Jasper Mellinger had been found. The county coroner held an inquest but no decision could be reached, and no case was ever presented to the county grand jury.

The sad relics were taken to the Roaring Fork area and were shown to Martha. There was no doubt; she recognized the rifle as the one Jasper had so often used to bring home meat for the table, and the watch had been his treasured possession. As was the custom, the men of the community gathered and built a coffin for the bones while the women kept Martha company in the house, and, on the appointed day, a sorrowful group escorted a wagon carrying the coffin to the family burial plot. A simple stone was erected over the grave and the remains of Jasper Mellinger lie there to this day.

But the question remained: How did Jasper die? No answers were forthcoming. With only herself to manage the farm, Martha could not support herself, and her son had all he could do to keep his family together. Eventually, Martha moved to the Sevier County Poor Farm and died there in 1925. By the time of her death, she had become very popular with both the residents of the farm and with the staff because of her pleasant disposition and modest ways. She was so well thought of that the Poor Farm staff took up money and provided a good coffin for her burial instead of the usual pine box made of locally cut boards. She was laid to rest in the paupers' field section of the Sevierville Cemetery.

Then a lead suddenly appeared. In the Wears Cove community a man named Beasley lay dying. There was something on his conscience he did not want to take with him to the grave. He was, he said, "going to see hell for the killing of Jasper Mellinger." So he called for his minister and his family and told this account. In 1901 he and his father, John Beasley, had gone into the mountains to hunt and to trap bears. Trapping of bears was illegal, but they had decided to run the risk of being caught violating the game laws. They placed their traps along game trails and planned to check them every day or so.

Now, let us go back to 1901 and Jasper Mellinger on his way to the Everett Mine in the Hazel Creek area.

Nearing the high crest of the main ridge, Jasper was following a game trail that had also been followed by occasional travelers, making it more distinct than a mere trace. Jasper knew just where he was and he knew he was on course for his destination. Then Jasper stepped over a log. There was a loud "snap" and terrible waves of pain swept up his leg. Immediately Jasper knew what had happened; he had stepped into a bear trap. These devices were illegal because they were such a danger to both livestock and to people, but someone had set one in a place where a bear was likely to pass and Jasper had been caught.

Opening the jaws of a bear trap requires the application of a great deal of pressure to the release lever. If Jasper had been able to stand upright he probably could have exerted enough pressure to open the trap; as it was, his leg was broken badly, the trap was anchored to a stake driven into the ground, and the chain was not long enough to allow him to stand. The intense pain and shock from his wound caused him to lose consciousness, for how long at a time he did not know. Even worse, the chance of anyone else coming along the trail was slight; Jasper had chosen a direct route but not a well-traveled one.

Taking inventory of his possessions Jasper found he had a little food, no water since he drank from the streams he crossed, and little hope. But he was tough. He would hang on as long as he could. The afternoon slowly passed, night fell, and the hours of darkness passed even more slowly and the pain in his leg only increased. By the next morning he was racked with fever as infection set in, and there were more frequent periods of unconsciousness that began to last longer and longer. Although Jasper was hardly aware of what was going on, hour followed hour and day followed day. His strength was ebbing fast, but then he heard footsteps. Someone was coming, perhaps two people. It was John Beasley and his son. They had neglected to check their trap for almost five days and now they faced the horrible fact that they had caught a man, a man who was almost dead. What were they to do? There did not seem to be much hope of getting their victim down the mountain and of saving his life. If they brought him back dead, how could they explain the matter? If he lived they would face criminal charges for setting an illegal trap and for endangering his life. One solution seemed obvious.

"You, boy! Pick up that stout stick yonder and knock that feller in the head. He's nigh done fer and it'll be a mercy to put him out of his misery." The then young Beasley could scarcely believe he was hearing his father say these words. Father and son argued. They hesitated, going over their options and the consequences facing them. At last, with great reluctance, the young man picked up a club and beat the remaining life out of Jasper Mellinger.

Together, they dragged the lifeless body off the trail and down the slope to the banks of a pool of water. There they covered the body with leaves and limbs broken from nearby hemlock trees. The rifle and pocket watch were valuable, but they were too easily recognized for them to risk taking with them, so they were left as well. The small amount of money Jasper was carrying was likely buttoned into one of the pockets of his bib-overalls and the Beasleys did not want to handle the corpse any more than was necessary, so no search was made of Jasper's person. Then they left and they kept quiet. This was the story told by the dying man.

Some of the local residents who remembered the disappearance of Jasper, and the discovery of his remains, were not persuaded by this confession. Jim Cate, a resident of the Elkmont area, felt the story was just that, a story. He had seen the bones recovered from the mountain and did not think there was evidence of a broken leg, certainly not the crushing of the bone a bear trap would have inflicted. There was evidence of a fracture, but it was high on the leg bone, not near the ankle where the jaws of a trap would have closed. There were others who agreed with Jim Cate and, eventually, Art Husky, another resident of the area, was accused of the crime.

This accusation produced a good deal of talk, but nothing came of it. Many people felt that the charge had been brought against Husky by people who did not like him and who were looking for any excuse to do him damage. Eventually the affair died away and the death of Jasper became a part of the folklore and traditional history of the area. But even today there are still questions to be answered.

Why did Mr. Beasley make a deathbed confession if his story was false? Why is the first name of the man who made the confession missing from all accounts and records of the event? Mysteries still linger about the event.

Did Jasper Mellinger step into a bear trap only to be killed several days later? Was he assaulted by an enemy whom he chanced to meet while crossing the mountains? Did he fall, break his leg, and then drag himself to the pool of water to slake his thirst only to die of infection and exposure some time later? The answer will never be known.

What is known is that the name of Mellinger was associated with the ridge as early as 1905. In 1943 the park and the US Geological Survey adopted the name "Mellinger Death Ridge" as the official designation for the location. Today the Greenbrier Ridge Trail takes hikers near the location of Jasper's death. This trail connects with the Appalachian Trail as it follows the high crest of the mountains, while the other end of the Greenbrier Trail is a junction with the Middle Prong Trail in the Hazel Creek drainage.

Not only hikers and folklorists are fascinated by the story of Jasper and his tragic death. The tragedy and mystery of the event has found expression well into the twenty-first century. In 2006 well-known singer/songwriter Jimmy Davis included a ballad about Mellinger Death Ridge on his album *Campfire Songs*.

Edward Mellinger, the son of Jasper and Martha, continued to live on the family farm until he sold the land to the park in 1929. The record of the sale shows the family lived in a two-room cabin and had a barn noted as being "in bad shape." Ed, as he was called, had seven children, grandchildren that Jasper never knew. He died in 1968 at the age of ninety-one, the last living direct connection to the tragic end of Jasper. Today the Mellinger Cemetery is accessible only by a manway, or unmaintained trail, which leads off the Roaring Fork Motor Nature Trail. The few visitors who make their way there will find the grave of Jasper and his two daughters.

Today millions of visitors come to Gatlinburg, drive into the park, and follow the Little River Road toward Elkmont, the route followed by Jasper Mellinger. They enjoy the sparkling waters of the river, marvel at the beauty of the wildflowers, and gape at the majesty of the Smokies towering along the high crest. Few are aware that looking back down on them is the ominously named Mellinger Death Ridge, site of a tragic death long before there was a park.

CHAPTER 2

A Mystery That Lasted Sixty Years: Edward McKinley

GEORGE MCKINLEY HAD A TEMPER; THAT FACT WAS WELL known throughout the community where he and his family lived. Their small house was located between the popular summer resort of Montvale Springs and Townsend. Montvale Springs had been a popular antebellum resort for the wealthy people of the region but was in decline by 1915. The McKinleys had no contact with the wealthy; they were poor. Perhaps George had such a quick temper because he had eleven children but few skills with which to support them, working as a logger for one of the local timber companies. The daily stress of hard work and scant economic reward would have done nothing to improve his outlook on life. All his children were strong willed, and this often caused them to be the objects of harsh discipline from their father.

Mary McKinley, George's wife, had learned that it was better to keep silent and express no opposition to George's outbursts. Such opposition simply focused his wrath on her. Some of the children, especially the girls, adopted the plan followed by their mother, but this did not prevent squabbles and bickering among the children. As soon as the girls were old enough, they began looking for husbands, and by 1915 two of them had married and had left home.

As was the case on any mountain farm, all the children had their chores. There was a garden to be tended, vegetables to be picked, water to be brought in from the well, eggs to be gathered, cows to be milked, butter to be churned; there was some productive work every child could do starting as early as age four or five. The older boys took turns sawing and splitting wood for the stove that heated the house.

This stove was not a large one; its top was less than three feet from the floor and it had only two eyes. To put wood in the stove for fuel, an iron handle was inserted into a loop on the eye, the eye lifted clear, and the fuel was pushed in before the eye was replaced. The problem with such small stoves was that the wood had to be split into rather small pieces. The fuel was quickly consumed and fresh wood had to be added frequently. This meant the person splitting wood needed to chop up a great deal in order to fill the box that held the reserve supply. Filling the wood box was a daily, often twice daily, chore.

On March 28, 1915, the boy responsible for chopping and bringing in wood for the stove was Edward, called by the family "Edd." Edd had not had a good relationship with his father for several weeks. Perhaps Edd was feeling the beginnings of adolescent rebellion and the need to assert his independence. Whatever the cause, he had several confrontations with his father as winter gave way to early spring and the result was always the same: Edd got a severe punishment.

Like many men of the time, George felt that if he supported his children and his wife they owed him complete, unquestioning, and instant obedience. Early on the morning of March 28, 1915, matters between Edd and George came to a crisis point.

Edd got up early and shivered as he put on his clothes in the cold house. As usual, their small stove had burned up all its fuel during the night and the fire had gone out. The house would not be warm until Edd got a fire going. Then he would need to hustle out to the wood pile where logs had been sawed into appropriate lengths, called "bolts." He would then take the ax and split these bolts into pieces and carry armloads into the house until he had filled the wood box with enough fuel to last the day. If the day was cold, the process would need to be repeated before sunset to provide fuel to heat the house during the early evening and to have some firewood on hand to start the fire the following morning.

On this particular day nothing went right. One of the pieces of firewood was too long and the eye would not go back on the stove. Cold, frustrated, wanting his breakfast but knowing it would not be ready anytime soon, Edd kicked the end of the stick of firewood. The wood did not go into the stove. Instead the stove tipped up on two legs, smoke, ashes, and a few live coals rolled out, and smoke filled the room. The scene was chaos. Fortunately, the stove was not yet hot and the family members were able to settle it back on all four legs, tap the stove pipe back together firmly, and get the hot coals into a shovel before any real damage was done. Not surprisingly, George flew into one of his fits of temper with Edd as the object of his anger. This time Edd stood his ground. Angry, harsh words were exchanged on both sides and then, to the surprise of all, George headed for the door. He had to get to work. He had no sooner closed the door behind him than he opened it again to tell Edd that when he got home that evening Edd would regret what he had said and done. It was obvious that a severe whipping was in the offing.

Mary McKinley tried to comfort her son after George had gone. She advised him that he should not talk back to his father since that only made matters worse, and she gave him a smile. Edd didn't respond in kind; he simply walked to the back door of the house and headed for the wood pile. Adding to his frustration, Edd found that the brother who had cut wood the day before had not sharpened the ax when he finished, so another step was added to his chores. He sat on the chopping block for a little while, holding the ax in one hand and the file in the other. Then putting down the ax and the file used to sharpen it, Edd went back into the house. Edd told some of his brothers and sisters that he was going to visit his grandmother Elizabeth McKinley who lived in Cherokee, North Carolina, on the other side of the mountains. He did not pack any extra clothes, and he took no food for the journey. Without even saying goodbye to his mother, Edd walked away from his home. None of the family would ever see him again.

When George came home he called for Edd, since he had every intention of carrying out his promise of punishment. Mary said she had not seen Edd since early that morning when he walked out to the wood pile. As darkness began to fall and suppertime drew near, the anxiety level of the family rose as Edd did not appear. The next day, and for a couple more days, the family looked around in the fields and woods near their house; they asked their neighbors, but no one had seen Edd. Finally, one of the brothers told Mary that Edd had said he was going to her mother's house. A general sense of relief flooded the family.

Edd had set out from home following the Little River upstream toward the Metcalf Bottoms area. From there he crossed over the end of Sugarlands Mountain, followed the course of Fighting Creek, and entered the Sugarlands community. Sugarlands was a good-sized mountain community. There was a store, a church, two gristmills, and three blacksmith shops. From Sugarlands a rough track, the Cherokee road or Indian Road, led up and over the mountains to Cherokee in North Carolina. Edd was a strong walker and he covered this considerable distance in a day. The Cherokee road had been laid out during the Civil War, but it had never been properly improved. Many of those traveling over the mountains did not attempt to use vehicles with wheels but built crude sleds or skids that oxen dragged over the rough road.

Late March and early April is a time when the weather in the Smokies can make violent and sudden changes. Warm air, pushing up from the Gulf of Mexico, can collide with a late spring surge of air coming down from the Arctic. The result can be sudden drops in temperature and heavy snowfall. Indeed, the heaviest snowfall of any season is likely to come at the end of winter, just as spring is on the doorstep. By the time Edd reached Sugarlands it was clear that such a weather event was in the making. A fine spring rain had turned icy as the temperature fell, and by late evening snow was falling steadily.

Edd stopped at the house of Bill Newman, warmed and dried himself at their fire, but declined their invitation to stay the night. It was still some time before dark and he wanted to put more miles behind him. Still later that day Edd came to the house of Riley Bracken and found the man of the house in the backyard chopping wood while his children carried it into the house. With snow coming down a good supply of dry, split wood in the wood box with extra stacked under cover on the back porch was desirable. Edd was invited to eat supper with the family and he accepted the invitation. To show his appreciation for the proffered hospitality, he helped carry in firewood.

After supper Edd was invited to stay the night, but his host suggested that all the boys, Edd included, make some additional trips to the wood pile for more firewood. This suggestion must have struck a raw nerve in Edd. To carry in wood in response to a kind invitation to eat a meal was a voluntary act; what he had just heard seemed too much like the orders his father was so fond of giving. Edd announced that he would just move on up the mountains and despite protests from the Bracken family, he left their house.

Now the story becomes confused. According to one account, the next morning the Bracken family awoke to see the ground covered deep in snow and icicles hanging from the eaves of their house. The temperature was very cold. They were worried about the young man who had eaten with them the night before, and Riley Bracken Jr. and a relative, Lev Trentham, agreed to go look for the stranger. A few hours later the two returned with a sad burden slung over their shoulders, the body of the boy who had been their guest the night before. But this account does not accord with the memories of other families in the area and there is another account of the tragedy.

The snow which had fallen on the preceding weekend had melted by Wednesday and Joe and Jim Cole, cousins, decided to go on a hunt. Wild greens, such as poke sallet, were beginning to come up and the women in their families intended to gather a good "mess" of greens. All winter the families had eaten salted pork and the idea of fresh greens touched off a longing for fresh meat. So Jim and Joe took their guns and set off. They intended to follow the Cherokee road up to the high crest, cross the ridge at Road Gap, and go on to the headwaters of Deep Creek in North Carolina. There were not many people out on the road, and they were anticipating their hunt when they saw a body propped under a leaning rock. The remains of a ring of stones and a collection of sticks indicated that he had tried to shelter himself under the rock and start a fire, but he had failed and had died of exposure.

The Coles had lived in the area all their lives and knew everybody in the vicinity, but this person was a stranger to them: a boy about twelve or so, red hair and freckles on his cheeks. Who was he? As they bore the body back down the mountain, Jim and Joe stopped at the cabin of Goldie Brown at Indian Grave Flats. Today this location is reached by taking the Chimney Tops trail for 0.9 mile to its junction with Road Prong Trail and turning uphill for a short distance. Mr. Brown recalled that the lad had stopped at his house just before darkness fell and he was invited to come in. He stayed about an hour, sitting beside the fire but then, despite the darkness and the snow, declared his intention of going on up the mountain. An urgent invitation to stay the night had been refused.

It was in the early hours of the morning when the Cole cousins arrived back at Sugarlands.

They found a sheltered place where the snow still lay in a drift and laid the body there to preserve it. For the next three days all the residents of the area who could came to view the body, but no one could identify the dead boy. The passage of time and the warming weather made it necessary for the remains to be buried, so the community rallied as they always did to meet the demands such an occasion presented. Two local men made a coffin of pine; the owner of the local store, David Ogle, donated clean clothes; a grave was dug in the Sugarlands Cemetery; and the unknown stranger was laid to rest with a large rock taken from the mountainside as a headstone.

But the story has several remaining twists. On April 14, 1915, on page two of *Montgomery's Vindicator*, published in the nearby town of Sevierville, there appeared a short note which read:

"A son of George McKinley who lives near Montvale Springs crossing over the smoky mountains during the recent snow storm was found a few days ago by Riley Brackens (sic) of this county just across the state line frozen to death."

If this news ever reached the Sugarlands community, no one made the connection between the unknown boy they had buried and this "son of George McKinley." Neither does it appear that Riley Bracken gave any additional information to his neighbors in nearby Sugarlands.

It was well known in the Sugarlands community that the Bracken family did not get along with the Cole family. There was a long-standing hostility between the two groups and fistfights between members of the families were not uncommon. There had been more serious violence on several occasions, including the exchange of gunfire. Three members of the Cole family had been killed by Riley Bracken. Perhaps this rivalry accounts for each family claiming to have found the body of Edd McKinley and for there being no attempt to reconcile the two accounts.

Today hundreds of thousands of visitors coming to visit the Great Smoky Mountains National Park pass through Sevierville, going on through Pigeon Forge, to Gatlinburg. If traffic is not heavy, the drive from the place where the newspaper was published to the location of the Sugarlands community takes only a few minutes. In 1915 things were quite different. The few roads were rough tracks, which alternated between mud holes and rocky outcrops. Travel was slow and difficult. Even more difficult was finding the time and money for travel. On a farm some work had to be done every day, regardless of the season—livestock must be fed and watered, cows must be milked, vegetables that are in season must be gathered and the surplus preserved for use in the winter. Money was very scarce for most people. Newspapers were considered a luxury, especially since postage had to be paid for their delivery in addition to the price of a subscription. Even if one subscribed to a paper, a visit to the local post office might not take place more than once a month.

So the news of the death of "A son of George McKinley" seems never to have reached Sugarlands to alert the residents of the possible identity of the lad they had buried. Instead, each Decoration Day when the community gathered to clean up the cemetery, the grave of the unknown was tended and flowers placed on it.

Just a few miles from the grave, at the home of George McKinley, the fate of their son and brother was never mentioned. Edd's name was banned from utterance and his memory became dim, although it did not vanish. Perhaps George felt guilt that he had driven his son into the snowy mountains to die; perhaps he was just not able to cope with his grief. But if George said no word about Edd, neither would the others.

So the mystery remained for many years. In 1936 the Great Smoky Mountains National Park was established. The Sugarlands community disappeared as families sold their farms and moved to other locations. But the cemetery remained and in it stood the simple rock marking the grave of the unknown lad whose life ended in 1915, and the memories of that event were still stored in the minds of some of those who had witnessed his burial.

In late May 1975, a woman in her mid-sixties came to the Sugarlands Visitors Center and asked to speak to someone who had worked in the park for a long time. She identified herself as Virgie Smith, the sister of Edd McKinley, and she was on a quest to determine if her brother was buried anywhere in the park. She lived in Knoxville and had resided in the area all her life. A discussion among the park employees caused one of them to remember a letter in the office files that had been sent them by Lucinda Ogle some years earlier. Apparently there had been a story about the lost boy incident and Mrs. Ogle, a longtime resident of the area and a member of one of the old families in the Smokies, had written an account of what she remembered of it. Although not all of the details fit what she remembered, this was the lead Virgie needed and a visit to the Ogle home was soon arranged. Like Virgie, the Ogles had not moved far away; they lived in Gatlinburg.

As Virgie and Lucinda talked over the events of long ago, it became clear to Virgie that the person buried in the grave marked "Unknown" was indeed her long-lost little brother. Although Virgie had only been about five years old when Edd left home, she remembered clearly his strongest identifying features, his thick red hair and his freckles. She also remembered that her mother, Mary McKinley, had never forgotten her lost son and had always grieved for him. Earnest Ogle, Lucinda's husband, also had strong memories of the event; he had helped dig the grave in which Edd was buried. Both of the Ogles remembered the red hair and freckles. Virgie and the Ogles had many visits and from those visits there came the decision to finish what had been begun so many years ago in Sugarlands.

Virgie began talking with the Park Service and with her family. Permission was granted for a permanent marker to be placed at the grave, and an appropriate tombstone was purchased for the grave and engraved with Edd's name along with the dates of his birth and death. The road to the Sugarlands Cemetery had long since become a walking trail so, on the day chosen for the event, one of Virgie's sons carried the grave marker on his back as a gesture of respect to the long-dead uncle he had never met. At last the mystery of the death of Edd McKinley had an ending.

Today the Sugarlands Cemetery is a peaceful place, visited by an occasional hiker or by a descendant of those hardy people who once inhabited these mountains. To reach the cemetery a hiker can park at the Sugarlands Visitors Center and walk across the lawn in the direction of Gatlinburg. At the bridge where the West Prong of the Little Pigeon River goes under the road, carefully cross to the far side of the road to find the trailhead. The Old Sugarlands Trail goes to the right at the point where a bridle path called the Twomile Branch Trail goes left. Watch for one more right turn at the point where the Twomile Lead Trail goes straight ahead, and soon one is walking in the flat bottomland near the river. This was the heart of the Sugarlands community. As you follow the still recognizable roadbed of the pre-park road, the Sugarlands Trail makes a sharp left turn. The level path that goes straight ahead at this point leads to the Sugarlands Cemetery and the now-marked grave of Edd McKinley.

CHAPTER 3

Survived the War But Not the Smokies

WHEN THE SECOND WORLD WAR BEGAN, THE US ARMY Air Corps expanded rapidly. Since the southern United States offered a climate suitable for flying year-round and because there was a large amount of open land available at reasonable prices, many air bases were established in the South, especially for training pilots and crews. In addition to air corps bases, the "Secret City" of Oak Ridge, Tennessee, just northwest of Knoxville, became a focal point of the Manhattan Project, the attempt to create an atomic bomb. In addition to the air traffic generated by training missions there would be a steady stream of passenger flights into Oak Ridge carrying scientists and engineers working on the bomb. There soon developed a nationwide network of bases with constant military travel going on between them. As a result, air traffic over the Smokies increased, and so did crashes. Some people escaped the dangers of the war only to perish in the Smokies.

One of the first fatal World War II era crashes in the Smokies involved Oak Ridge. On January 31, 1944, at 9:42 a.m., a Cessna training plane capable of carrying both crew and passengers left Charlotte, North Carolina, bound for Lebanon, Tennessee, on an administrative flight. The pilot was Second Lieutenant Irving Bumberg of New York City. Accompanying him as passengers were First Lieutenant Thomas Wheeler, who was stationed at Morris Field in Charlotte, First Lieutenant George Marty, and Dr. Carlton Haigis, of Greenfield, Massachusetts. Dr. Haigis was fifty-one years old and had had an interesting career in science. In 1917 and 1918 Haigis had been associated with early rocket science researcher Dr. Robert H. Goddard. Later Dr. Haigis had been the chief physicist for the Victor Talking Machine Company. During this time he became interested in the science and technology of radios and developed the original walkie-talkie communications devices used by the US armed forces. In 1944 Dr. Haigis was employed by the US Army as an operations analyst.

After leaving Charlotte the plane was reported near Bryson City and Fontana Dam. Several of the people who said they had seen the plane stated that the engine was not running smoothly, sputtering and popping, and that it seemed to be very low, too low to make it across the high peaks of the Smokies looming just ahead, obscured by snow and fog.

It appears that the crash took place in the middle of the day, but reports of the possible accident did not reach authorities until late in the afternoon. Preparations for a thorough search were begun on January 31, and the next morning an air search was undertaken. Since there was no precise location for the crash, the available planes had to cover a very large area and no positive results were reported. A new piece of technology was brought in to help in the mission, a helicopter, but its crew found nothing.

With no clues to follow, the air search wound down in a few days, although relatives of some of the missing men kept up a search for some time. Two years later remains of a plane were found by a hunter near Maggie Valley, several miles from the last possible sightings reported in 1944. On August 10, 1946, local papers reported that a three-man search party headed by Captain James B. Greene had found the crash site. A larger team was dispatched to the site, and the next day it was reported that the bodies of the missing men had been found. The remains of Dr. Haigis were taken to Shelburne Falls, Massachusetts, and were buried in the family plot there.

For some reason there is disagreement among those who remember and are interested in this crash. Several sources say the wreckage was never discovered and the bodies never recovered, yet the online biography of Dr. Haigis reveals his gravesite.

—◆—

During the period between the world wars many people became fascinated with flying, some of them enough so that they went to great lengths to earn a pilot's license. One of these was A. E. "Eddie" Leonard of Charlotte, North Carolina. Eddie was a natural as a pilot and soon was making a living as a stunt flier with traveling air shows. He also took students and taught flying lessons.

When World War II came along, Eddie became a flight instructor for the Army Air Corps and then was stationed at McGhee Tyson Airport at Knoxville as a pilot for the scientists working at Oak Ridge, the "Secret City." The aircraft used to transport the scientists was one of the most advanced civilian planes of the day, a Beechcraft Staggerwing, a plane with an enclosed cabin and an extensive range. Airplane designer T. A. Wells and aircraft executive Walter H. Beech had designed the Beechcraft in the early 1930s. It was a large, powerful, and fast biplane with an enclosed cabin, designed to appeal to business executives. When World War II began the US Army Air Corps ordered several of these craft, model UC-43, to use as transport and courier planes. The aircraft was comfortable for passengers and had an excellent safety record.

Riding in the Staggerwing was another pilot, Shelby Ray Parham, of Monroe County, Mississippi. Shelby, born in 1920, was one of the generation between the wars who was fascinated by flying. Although from a rural area of Mississippi and a member of a large family with seven children, Shelby had learned to fly and had become an instructor for US Army pilot cadets at Charlotte, North Carolina. He was remembered as an excellent instructor who took a keen interest in his students, although he was very strict with them. He also dressed formally, in a suit and tie, for every lesson and practice flight. Shelby worked as a flight instructor until sometime in 1943 and then was employed at Oak Ridge as one of their pilots.

A third passenger in the Staggerwing was Reuben Johnson, an airplane mechanic. The three men were to fly from McGhee Tyson Airport in Knoxville to Charlotte and, following a short stop, go on to Pittsburgh. The plane took off at a little past 10:00 a.m. on August 12, 1944. The aircraft never arrived in Charlotte, so a search was instituted. For more than two weeks, people looked from the air and on the ground for the missing plane and its passengers. There had been reports from people on the ground of a plane flying low that appeared to have engine trouble, but no locations were given that might lead to a crash site. Such fruitless searches are always an emotional drain on those participating in them but, at last, it was agreed they had done all they could do and the search was closed down.

Twenty-nine months went by. The war ended and a grateful nation returned to peace. The Great Smoky Mountains National Park began to attract more visitors, among them the members of the Smoky Mountain Hiking Club, an organization that predates the founding of the park and whose members enjoy going off the trails into the backcountry of the park. This club planned a hike to an area known as "Wooly Tops," in the park's Greenbrier section, an area known for steep rock bluffs and plunging cascades.

On January 19, 1947, a hiker from this group discovered physical remains of the missing plane. When Park Service personnel, accompanied by members of the Leonard family, followed up on this report, they found serial numbers on the wreckage matching the missing plane. An extensive search found no evidence of human remains.

Today, in the New Hope Cemetery in Monroe County, Mississippi, there is a small marker whose inscription reads: "Shelby Parham 1920–1944. Lost in Plane Crash Blue Ridge Mtns.," a touching reminder of men who gave their lives, not in combat, but in the service of their country during World War II.

By October 1945 the combat phase of World War II had ended with the surrender of Japan following the use of two atomic bombs. The "Secret City" of Oak Ridge, just outside the park, had played a major role in developing the weapons that brought about the surrender. But the United States still had hundreds of thousands of servicemen, and servicewomen, to process for discharge while retaining many others for occupation duties in Europe and Asia. Some of these service personnel, having survived the war, became tragic victims of death in the Smokies while on their way home.

On October 5, 1945, First Lieutenant Robert Barton got behind the controls of a C-45 military transport plane at Cincinnati for a flight to Charlotte, North Carolina. Four passengers and one crewmember boarded the plane with him. The other crewmember was the crew chief, not a pilot. The four passengers had completed their service and were on their way home: W. R. Haines, Hollis Brobrick, Stanley Lerner, and one young woman, Lena E. Allred, a member of the Women Accepted for Volunteer Emergency Service (WAVEs). The WAVEs were an official US Navy organization formed in 1942 to provide more personnel for behind-the-lines duties in order to free more men to go to the fighting front. The WAVEs held rank just as men did. By the end of the war, twenty-seven thousand young women had enlisted in the WAVEs.

Just before 5:00 p.m. Lieutenant Barton received clearance for takeoff with instructions to cruise at five thousand feet. The plane was expected to arrive in Charlotte about 7:30 p.m. The altitude of five thousand feet was a problem, because the route to be followed led over the high crest of the Great Smoky Mountains where peaks reach well above six thousand feet. Shortly after takeoff the tower at Cincinnati gave new instructions; Lieutenant Barton was to fly at seven thousand feet. For reasons now unknown this was not done and the flight continued at five thousand feet.

As the flight path took the airplane closer to the Smoky Mountains, weather conditions deteriorated with heavy clouds and intervals of rain. It may be that Lieutenant Barton became confused as he began to see mountains reaching higher than he was flying, but it seems he made a turn to the left. Perhaps he was looking for a hole in the clouds; maybe he intended to make a 180-degree turn and go back to McGhee Tyson Field at Knoxville. Whatever he meant to do, he flew straight into the side of 6,003-feet-high Mount Sequoya.

When the plane had not arrived in Charlotte in a reasonable time, all military airfields near its route were contacted to see if weather or mechanical trouble had caused a landing there; all responses were negative. Early on the morning of October 7, search proceedings began. One problem was there was no "last known position" on which to base the search; the plane could be anywhere between Cincinnati and Charlotte. It was several days before the search began to home in on the Great Smokies, and then the initial search was directed toward other areas of the park, based on reports from people on the ground who had heard low-flying planes. A search plane flying over Mount Sequoya finally spotted the wreckage on October 14. Foot search teams were immediately sent in by the Park Service.

The weather was wet and intensely cold, but the teams followed the Appalachian Trail to a point as close as possible to the crash site and then bushwhacked their way down the slope to the wreckage. All the bodies were found and a tremendous effort was put into carrying the remains to the Appalachian Trail. For a long distance the search party had to carry their burden of human remains up a slope estimated to be sixty-six degrees, a slope almost impossible to walk on even if both hands are free to help. At the trail horses were waiting to carry the bodies the rest of the way to a road. In this, as in all cases, the remains were handled with the greatest possible dignity and reverence.

Earlier World War II crashes in the park had involved civilian aircraft being used by the US Army; this was the first crash of a true military plane. Lena Allred was the first woman to be killed in an air crash in the park. She was buried with full military honors in Richmond County, North Carolina, in the Eastside Cemetery.

The toll of aircraft had not yet been paid in full. The largest airplane then in use, a B-29 Superfortress, was about to have a date with destiny in the Smoky Mountains. The B-29 Superfortress was a heavy bomber designed by the Boeing Corporation with four engines, a pressurized cabin, and an electronic fire-control system that coordinated the guns in four machine gun turrets. There was another gun position in the tail of the aircraft, but it was manned.

The United States began to deploy these bombers in May 1944, and they would continue in service until June 1960.

The B-29 was among the most technologically advanced planes produced during the Second World War.

MacDill Field at Tampa, Florida, was the base for part of the nation's bomber fleet. From MacDill it was common for crews to be sent on round-trip flights to Chicago in order to hone navigation skills. Such a trip was assigned to a twelve-man crew on June 11, 1946, and they made the trip to Chicago without incident. At 2:16 a.m. on June 12, the radio operator on the bomber, Sergeant Charles E. Bausch, made radio contact with the airfield at Knoxville, a routine check-in on the way back to Tampa. Not long after that a policeman in Sevierville reported that he heard a large plane going over at an altitude he thought to be too low to clear the mountains, but no report was made of anything else. Park Superintendent Blair Ross later said the weather was not at all unusual for the time of year, although fog and low clouds often built up over the highest peaks of the mountains.

In the early morning of June 12, a park maintenance crew was driving up the road from Newfound Gap to Clingmans Dome. The driver of their vehicle rounded a curve about three-quarters of a mile short of the Dome and slammed on his brakes. In the road lay a huge aircraft engine, and on the left, or North Carolina side, there was a long and wide swath of trees sheared off not far above the ground. A quick look down the slope revealed a massive debris field. The Park Service men quickly returned to Newfound Gap, blocked off the road, and called for help.

There was no need for a search this time. The giant aircraft had hit the main ridge of the Smokies on the Tennessee side, apparently with its nose up. Perhaps the pilots did not even see the mountain until they were almost at the point of impact and then tried to lift the nose of the plane up over it. They failed by only a few feet. On the Tennessee side of the road the plane had crashed through the trees for several yards, shearing off both its wings, then hit a large boulder and bounced back into the air. The fuselage of the bomber bounced over the Clingmans Dome road and struck the ground for its final disintegration, killing the crew instantly. All the bodies of the crew were found on the North Carolina side of the road.

Military officials soon arrived on the scene to recover the bodies of the airmen, and over the next several days several instruments whose design and operation were classified as "secret" were removed from the wreckage. While twelve lives were lost in this tragic accident, perhaps radio operator Charles Bausch's story is the most poignant. He was twenty years old and had enlisted in the Air Corps in January 1944. His term of enlistment was over on June 13, and this was his last flight in service to his country. Sergeant Bausch was from Bettendorf, Iowa.

~ ~

The last air crash of the Second World War era took place on September 13, 1946, just outside the park boundary, in Haywood County, North Carolina, in what is today the Shining Rock Wilderness of Pisgah National Forest, adjacent to the Great Smoky Mountains National Park. This was another flight from MacDill Air Force Base in Tampa to Detroit, Michigan, where one of the passengers, Major General Paul D. Wurtsmith, was to make a routine inspection of the facilities. General Wurtsmith had just recently been named temporary commander of the Eighth Air Force. The plane, a B-25 bomber, carried a crew of five and two passengers. A stop was made in Washington, DC, so General Wurtsmith could attend to some official business, and the two passengers left the plane at that point; the remaining five men soon continued to Detroit.

The general was a native of Detroit, and he used the overnight hours to visit with his family. The return trip to Tampa began at just after 9:00 a.m. on September 13. The flight plan listed General Wurtsmith as the pilot. About 11:00 a.m. radio contact was made with the airport serving Johnson City, Tennessee, and the bomber reported bad weather closing in and requested to be assigned an altitude below six thousand feet. The traffic controller replied that the mountains ahead would require a higher altitude and that the plane was advised to ascend. A response came back from the bomber that the pilot now had visual control and did not need instrument control, so the lower altitude was maintained. Less than thirty minutes later the aircraft hit the top of Cold Mountain, sheared off the tops of trees in a large area, and smashed into a cliff. All aboard were killed instantly.

The area around the crash site had not yet been made a part of the public land that now includes the Smokies and Pisgah Forest, so many people lived in the vicinity. The noise of the explosion when the plane struck the ground announced that something bad had taken place, and people began to investigate. In that rural area telephones were not common, so the investigation consisted of people going into the woods, up the mountain, then returning to tell others of what they had found. Soon the news reached a cross-roads store where a telephone was available, and authorities were notified. Beginning on September 15 military personnel secured the area, removing the bodies and searching the wreckage for any items that might be of importance to the Air Corps. When they were finished word was spread that anything remaining could be taken by anyone who wanted it. Several people secured pieces of the aluminum skin of the plane or other such small reminders of the tragedy.

Major General Paul Wurtsmith, the son of a German immigrant, had joined the US Army in 1928. He soon became an expert pilot and rose to the pre-war rank of captain. Not long after the Japanese attack on Pearl Harbor, Captain Wurtsmith was sent to the Philippines and, in the fighting there, was promoted to major and, in only nine months, to lieutenant colonel and full colonel. In recognition of his skill and tenacity in leading his men against the enemy, he was promoted to brigadier general at age thirty-six. Some of the hardest fighting Wurtsmith did was in defending Darwin, Australia, in early 1942 as the Japanese followed up their initial successes in the Pacific by pushing toward that target. Outnumbered and flying slower planes, Wurtsmith led his men in a successful defense of Darwin and then took part in the slow recovery of territory by the Allied forces beginning in 1943. By 1945 he was in command of the 13th Air Force, operating out of the reoccupied Philippines against Japanese targets in French Indochina, as Vietnam was then called. Even when promoted to major general, Wurtsmith always "led from the front," setting an example by going himself where he expected his men to go.

A second combat veteran who died in the crash was Lieutenant Colonel Fred Trickey Jr., an "army brat" who grew up on army bases and followed his father into a military career. Trickey dropped out of college to join the army in 1940 and soon qualified as a pilot. During the first years of the conflict, he was a member of the Transport Command, ferrying airplanes from the United States to North Africa. Later he flew planes to Australia, but in late 1944 he was assigned to a combat role and began to fly bombers attacking the home islands of Japan. On one of these missions, his plane was heavily hit and lost two engines, both on the same side. Although advised by other pilots in his flight to ditch the plane and bail out, Trickey performed an astounding feat of flying, bringing his craft and crew safely back to their base. For this feat he was awarded the Silver Star.

The loss of any life is tragic, but it seems especially so in the cases of Lena Allred, Paul Wurtsmith, and Fred Trickey Jr. They had survived World War II, but they did not survive the Smokies.

CHAPTER 4

Not Dead Despite the Odds

ON JANUARY 15, 2009, US AIRWAYS FLIGHT 1549 TOOK OFF from LaGuardia Airport in New York City for a flight to Charlotte, North Carolina. There were 155 passengers and crew aboard the aircraft. Some three minutes into the flight, at 3:27 p.m., the plane flew through a flock of Canada geese, and birds were sucked into both of the plane's engines. Seeing that it would be impossible to reach the nearest airfield, Captain Chesley B. Sullenberger decided to put the plane down in the Hudson River. With a great deal of skill, and a large measure of good luck, "Sully" Sullenberger put the plane in the water intact. All passengers and crew evacuated the aircraft and were rescued by boats. Only one person required hospitalization overnight; the rest were uninjured or only slightly injured. It was the only time in the history of US aviation that a passenger jet made a water landing with no fatalities. Captain Sullenberger became an instant national hero.

Oddly enough, there is a connection with this event and an airplane crash in the Great Smoky Mountains National Park.

Dr. Samuel Sullenberger was known as "the flying country doctor." Dr. Sullenberger owned a medical clinic in Dandridge, Tennessee, a small town just a few miles north of the eastern end of the Great Smoky Mountains National Park. Country doctors were not wealthy people in those days, but Dr. Sullenberger loved flying for the sense of relaxation, serenity, and peace it brought him. Flying was the hobby he pursued to escape the tension and long hours of his medical practice. In the fall of 1955, Dr. Sullenberger had purchased a new bright yellow Piper J-3, a model commonly called "the Colt." This was a very reliable plane with a top speed of 87 miles per hour and a range of three hundred miles.

On November 2, 1955, Dr. Sullenberger took off from the local airport in Dandridge and flew west to McGhee Tyson Airport, which serves Knoxville. Then he turned east and southeast to fly across the Smoky Mountains. He hoped to find a place to get some good pictures of the mountains, where much of the fall foliage was still intact. The doctor had told his wife to expect him home by 5:30 since it would be getting dark by that time, and when he did not arrive she phoned both the local airfield and McGhee Tyson field. The doctor was not at either of these places. His wife promptly reported him missing, but the darkness prevented any search from getting under way that day so the hours were spent planning for the next day when the sun rose.

The primary force used to locate the downed plane would be the Civil Air Patrol (CAP), then a decade-old organization that had worked with the National Park Service a few times in locating crashes on park property. The doctor had once been a member of the CAP. Of course, it was not known just where Dr. Sullenberger might have come down, so the CAP would have to search a large area. The only clue was a phone call from the community of Del Rio, Tennessee, that a small plane had been seen flying low over Morgans Gap and that the observer thought the plane might have crashed, although no smoke had been seen. On November 3, a clear day, more than two dozen planes flew back and forth across the area where the crash might have taken place, but they saw nothing.

As he was ready to turn for home on November 2, Dr. Sullenberger heard his engine begin to sputter. Thinking that the problem was probably caused by icing in the carburetor, he began to descend to find warmer air. Before his move was successful, he lost all power and the next best hope was to keep the plane aloft long enough to clear the mountain ridges and glide to a better area for a landing. A downdraft put an end to that hope, and the doctor braced himself as trees rushed up to meet him.

Dr. Sullenberger regained consciousness rapidly following the crash. Quickly taking inventory of his physical condition, the doctor was quite pleased to find that he had a small cut on his head but no other injuries. His plane had come to rest in the top of a tree and the branches had cushioned the impact so thoroughly that the propeller of the plane was not broken and the windows were not even damaged. The first problem confronting him was that he was several feet off the ground. The second problem was that a search of the cockpit revealed he had only a bag of peanuts and a can of sardines available for food. The third problem was that he did not really know where he was. Actually, the doctor was on

Mount Guyot, a 6,621-foot-high peak in the eastern end of the Great Smokies park, in one of the most remote sections of the park. The Appalachian Trail and the Balsam Mountain Trail intersect near Mount Guyot at Tricorner Knob, and these are the only two developed trails in the area. The site of Dr. Sullenberger's crash was indeed in a wilderness area.

The night was cold and his stomach growled a lot, but Dr. Sullenberger felt sure a search would be mounted for him as soon as there was enough light. With an intact bright yellow airplane sitting in the top of a tree, he did not think a search mounted by the pilots he knew in the CAP could miss him, and then it would be just a question of time before rangers appeared. But as the day grew brighter his frustration mounted as he saw low-flying planes flying over his location, obviously searching for something, but time after time these planes failed to see either his crashed aircraft or his frantic signals to them. So Dr. Sullenberger made a decision; if the searchers would not come to him, he would go to the searchers.

Since he was unsure of his location, the doctor followed one of the basic rules of survival—walk downhill; if you find a stream, keep it in sight or sound as you go down the slope. It was only a short time until Dr. Sullenberger found one of the tributaries of Big Creek, and he began to follow it down the mountains, going basically in an easterly direction. Fortunately, this stream led to the head of Big Creek Trail, and he had a marked route to follow and a reasonably good footway. When night came he curled up at the base of a tree, raked leaves over him, and slept as much as he could. During the day he had eaten the bag of peanuts, but they did little to ease his growing hunger.

Early on the morning of November 5, Dr. Sullenberger again set off. He was so hungry he decided to consume the one remaining item of food he had, the can of sardines. Fortunately, the can could be opened with a key attached to the can, and the doctor was soon savoring the strong-smelling little fish. Strong-smelling is a key word. The scent of the sardines caught the attention of a black bear cub, and soon there was a thrashing in the bushes as the cub waddled up to the doctor and made a grab for the can of sardines. Hungry as he was, Sullenberger was not inclined to give up his meal, scanty as it was, so he kicked the bear cub. The cub gave out a snort, which apparently was a distress call because Momma Bear came out of the surrounding woods in a hurry. Now Dr. Sullenberger faced an entirely new threat to his life. The sow bear was not so much interested in the sardines as she was in protecting her cub from attack, and she responded in a predictable fashion: She went right for the doctor.

Fortunately for Sullenberger, the cub was scuttling back into the bushes behind its mother so the attack was not pushed too hard. Yells and some blows with his fists prevented Dr. Sullenberger from being seriously injured, but he did receive a deep gash across his abdomen when the bear swiped at him with her claws.

The rush of adrenalin helped the doctor continue his downhill route once the bears had gone their way. He continued walking until he came to a welcome sight indeed, smoke rising from the chimney of the Big Creek Ranger Station. Knocking on the door, Dr. Sullenberger was greeted by the wife of the ranger. Of course she knew a search was going on for a crashed airplane, but no one had given her the name of the missing pilot, and she did not know who the doctor was. She did see he had a serious scratch across his middle, so she asked him in and got the first aid kit. When she asked what caused the cut Dr. Sullenberger blurted out, "Well, a bear did that but I have been in an airplane crash and I am awfully hungry." A radio call to the ranger and some fast work by his wife in the kitchen soon had the doctor on his way to park headquarters from where a phone call had already gone to his wife telling her he was alive and in good condition.

Dr. Sullenberger was taken to his own clinic in Dandridge, and his bear wound was treated there. A couple days rest and the doctor was again back in the office, treating patients and, no doubt, answering all sorts of questions about his experience. But his airplane was still up in a tree in a remote part of the Smoky Mountains.

As a former member of the CAP, Dr. Sullenberger appreciated all the hard work the members of that organization had done in searching for him. Some hours after he had left the site of the crash, two CAP members had spotted the downed plane and had reported the crash site. In gratitude for the effort they had made on his behalf, Dr. Sullenberger donated his plane to the CAP. The gift was much appreciated until a basic question was raised—how to get the craft down from the tree and then haul it out of the mountains? The more the matter was discussed, the more it seemed to be beyond the abilities of the CAP to perform. Eventually the plane was donated to another organization, who sent in a crew to disassemble the craft and haul it out of the park.

But how was the crash of a Piper Cub in the Great Smoky Mountains National Park in 1955 connected to the splash-down of US Airways Flight 1549 in the Hudson River in 2009?

The year before Dr. Sullenberger crashed his plane, he and his son had flown in an air race to California. Along the way they spent one night in Denison, Texas, at the home of one of Dr. Sullenberger's cousins who was a dentist in that town. During that evening Dr. Samuel Sullenberger met for the first time a three-year-old cousin he had never seen before. The name of the young fellow was Chesley B. Sullenberger.

Not dead, despite the odds. Good aviation luck seems to follow the family.

⁓

The same combination of skill and good luck was with the McCarra family of Mississippi in 1974.

It does not snow often in Mississippi, especially along the Gulf Coast where Ray and Phyllis McCarra lived with their three children, Jonathan, Jeffrey, and Noel. So when the weather forecast predicted a good chance of snow for Gatlinburg on the north edge of the Great Smoky Mountains National Park, Ray called his brother, Russell, and his wife Zilla and the seven of them planned a trip to the mountains to see the snow. Ray was a licensed pilot and his company owned a Cherokee Six, so the family decided to make the trip in the company aircraft. On February 16, 1974, the combined families took off from Pascagoula, Mississippi, with plans to travel to Chattanooga, Tennessee, stop for a few minutes, and then continue their trip to Sevierville, Tennessee, north of the park. From Chattanooga they could have flown northeast toward Knoxville and then turned toward Sevierville, or they could take the "scenic route" and fly over the main ridge of the Great Smoky Mountains to reach their destination. Since the weather looked quite good, Ray made the decision to fly over the mountains.

As the McCarra families approached the mountains, the cold front that was bringing the snow they had come to see was also arriving. The north wind was pushing across the lower elevations of eastern Tennessee and, when it met the mountains, was flowing upward like a river and then was spilling down into North Carolina. This condition is called an orographic lift and it is common in several areas in the United States, including the Great Smoky Mountains. As the air mass is forced from a low to a higher elevation by passing over rising terrain, the air cools quickly and the humidity rises, producing rain or snow. Transylvania County, North Carolina, just southeast of the park, gets more rain (ninety inches annually) than any other part of the eastern United States. This cooling and higher humidity was soon to cause serious problems for the McCarras.

As their plane began to pass over the highest peaks of the Smokies, ice began to form in the carburetor and the craft lost power, downdrafts began to toss the plane about the sky, and Ray was faced with a hard decision he needed to make quickly: Should he try to put the airplane down while he still had some control or should he turn back and risk an uncontrolled crash before he could get out of the mountains? Ray took the first option. His brother, Russell, was also a pilot, so the two worked together to bring their aircraft to a safe landing in the rough terrain below them.

Using their combined strength they managed to bring the plane to the ground in a "pancake" landing in which they intentionally stalled the engine and dropped to the ground in approximately horizontal fashion with little forward motion. The brothers pulled it off, but just by a hair. The nose of the plane smashed into a huge boulder, but the passenger cabin remained intact.

Ray's first thoughts were certainly for his three children, the youngest three years old and the oldest nine, and for his wife. He then quickly checked with Russell and Zilla, and found, to his great relief, that no one was hurt. The families knew the night would be cold, but they had coats in their suitcases so they bundled up, built a fire, and settled down in the wrecked cabin to keep as warm as they could and, perhaps, to snatch a little sleep. In the distance they could see occasional gleams of light but the source was clearly miles away. Morning brought light by which to see but nothing else of help. No one was expecting them in Sevierville so there would be no report of their not arriving there and, consequently, no search beginning immediately. It was clear to Ray that the best hope of survival for the group was for someone to walk out and find help, and he was the youngest and most fit. Ray then began an epic hike.

Off-trail hiking in the Smokies is very much like bushwhacking through a tropical jungle. The vegetation can be so thick that it is necessary to detour around thickets rather than force one's way through them, slopes can suddenly become very steep, and streams can suddenly leap over sheer bluffs. Ray encountered all of these obstacles and more as he worked his way downhill from the crash site, but he did have the good luck to find a trail along the shores of Fontana Lake. The signpost at the trail pointed the way to Clingmans Dome, a well-visited site in the park with which Ray was familiar. The problem was that the distance from Fontana Lake to Clingmans Dome was all uphill. Ray had had no food for hours and his energy level was low, but he was driven on by the knowledge that the survival of his family depended on him, so on he went.

Unknown to Ray, as he slogged uphill from Fontana Lake, he passed within a mile of the location of his family. If he had gone uphill when he left that morning instead of going downhill toward the lake he could have been at Clingmans Dome in two or three miles, but he had followed the common sense rule of going downhill. Finally Clingmans Dome loomed ahead, but on reaching it the parking lot was empty: not only empty but there were no tire tracks. The road to the Dome is closed in the winter. Ray did recall that this road ended at Newfound Gap, eight miles east. The Gap was on the Trans-Mountain Road from Gatlinburg, Tennessee, to Cherokee, North Carolina, and his hopes of finding help there were greater. But there was the challenge of distance and time. As weak as he was feeling, how long would it take to cover the eight miles? Obviously, he would be arriving there well into the night, so how long would it be before he could find help? Clearly, his family would have to spend another cold, hungry night in the woods.

Luck was with Ray. Late as it was when he arrived at Newfound Gap, he saw the lights of an approaching car. The driver gave him a ride and they happened upon a ranger who was patrolling the park roads. Now Ray had help and communications. Ray was taken to park headquarters where he told his full story and rangers began to plot the probable area where his plane had gone down.

A call was placed to the Civil Air Patrol emergency service so an air search could begin the next morning. The Park Service used the remaining hours of the night to send four rangers by jeep to Clingmans Dome who then hiked out to a shelter on the Appalachian Trail near where the crash was thought to have occurred. As soon as the sun had burned off the morning mist and there was light enough to see in the mountains, the CAP search planes took off. In less than a quarter of an hour one of the search planes spotted the crash site, and the crew was overjoyed to see six people waving up to them; everyone had survived the cold night. The crash had taken place less than two miles from Clingmans Dome, which meant Ray had hiked two-thirds of his distance in the wrong direction.

A second small plane dropped food, blankets, and more clothes to the survivors, and rangers began to hike in on foot. By noon rescuers had reached the McCarra families and it was determined that Ray's wife and children could walk out on their own power but Zilla needed some medical attention. The rangers split into teams to see to each of these tasks. By the middle of the night Ray and his family were reunited in Gatlinburg, but Zilla proved to be a more difficult case to handle. There was no helicopter available that could handle an air evacuation, so more supplies and warm sleeping bags were delivered to Zilla and Russell and the rangers who had stayed with them. For them, it would be another night in the park.

The following day brought deteriorating weather, but a large Chinook helicopter was brought in to make the attempt to lift out the party. Even this large, two-engine machine was no match for the weather, and the attempt at an air rescue was abandoned in mid-afternoon as thickening clouds obscured the crash area. Now it was time for swift action and hard work. A path was cleared up Devils Courthouse Ridge to the Appalachian Trail and eighty persons, rangers and volunteers, took their places along it. Relays of carriers bore Zilla up the mountain, east along the Appalachian Trail, and to the parking lot at Clingmans Dome. A waiting ambulance took Zilla to a hospital in Knoxville. There it was found she had serious but non-life-threatening internal injuries. Following treatment she and Russell were able to return home in several days.

❧

Not dead despite the odds. Dr. Samuel Sullenberger survived his crash and walked out of the park. All seven members of the McCarra party survived their crash, and six of them walked out under their own power while the seventh was able to resume normal activities in a relatively short time. Accidents can put people in very difficult places, but determination, good luck, and a lot of help from the Park Service and civic-minded citizens give some of these stories a happy ending.

CHAPTER 5

The Mysterious Disappearance of Dennis Martin

SPENCE FIELD IN MID-JUNE IS ONE OF THE LOVELIEST SPOTS in the Great Smoky Mountains National Park. The skies are clear most of the time with only a few cumulus clouds dotted here and there. Wide vistas stretch away in all directions; flame azalea, rhododendron, and mountain laurel display their blossoms along with numerous wildflowers. The high elevation, forty-five hundred feet, makes for pleasant daytime temperatures and provides just enough coolness at night to encourage a camper to snuggle into a sleeping bag. Spence Field is a popular hiking destination and backcountry camping spot, but huge crowds do not gather there. A backcountry shelter and a spring are the only accommodations. Spence Field is atop the high crest of the Smokies and is reached by hiking uphill for three and a half miles on the Anthony Ridge Trail and then following the Bote Mountain Trail for a little over a mile to reach the "bald" known as Spence Ridge. According to an often told story, a group of Cherokee road builders in the 1850s were asked to choose the route to follow up the mountains. The "v" sound is not part of the speech pattern of native Cherokee speakers, so the decision was reached by a "bote" instead of a "vote."

In the Smoky Mountains a "bald" is a mountaintop largely devoid of trees but covered by grass and shrubs. How and why an area becomes a bald is an ecological mystery, but it is agreed that grazing livestock on these meadows in pioneer times helped keep them open. Today the balds provide the best viewpoints of the surrounding mountains because of the absence of trees.

Considering the natural beauty of the location, it is no wonder that the Martin family of Knoxville, Tennessee, made an annual camping trip to Spence Field a Father's Day tradition. Indeed, this was part of a family tradition dating back to a time before the founding of the park.

Early in the twentieth century, John and Jim Martin were operators of a sawmill in the Anthony Creek area. The family owned a farm in the Little River area and drove their cattle up the Bote Mountain road every summer to allow the livestock to graze on the bald at Spence Field. There was no need to keep a daily check on the cattle, and they were left to fend for themselves except for a visit in mid-June when salt blocks were carried to the pasture.

After the park was established, the Martin family continued to hold something of an open-air family reunion at Spence Field each June. A dozen or more members of the Martin family—men, women, and children—would make the hike and enjoy the outdoors as well as each other's company.

The trip to Spence Field for 1969 was a special time because Clyde Martin, a Knoxville schoolteacher, would be accompanied not only by his adult son, Bill Clyde, but by Bill's two children, Doug and Dennis. Doug was nine years old and had made the trip before, but this would be the first time grandfather Clyde had enjoyed the company of six-year-old Dennis on the annual expedition. Dennis was a special education student, but he was healthy, strong, and had been on many day hikes with the family. In addition, Clyde's three brothers and a sister would be joining the party along with members of their families.

Clyde led his party up the Anthony Creek Trail to its junction with the Russell Field Trail and then on to the shelter at Russell Field to spend their first night in the mountains, and the next day the group made the short hike on to Spence Field where the rest of the group had been camping for a day or so. Not much was seen of wildlife as the group hiked along, although they did see one young black bear and, later, a sow bear with two cubs. Some of the hikers thought these bears were acting too familiar, as if they had come to associate people with food. This was, and is, one of the most serious problems in the park when it comes to managing wildlife and people. Wildlife usually shy away from people, but if the animals are fed by humans they begin to lose their fear of people and may become aggressive. This is particularly a problem with bears, which are quite fond of human food. Feeding bears always causes problems, sometimes for the person doing it, always for the bear, and often for both!

But, except for swatting gnats, there was no problem with wildlife and the hikers reached Spence Field and united with the rest of the Martin group. After lunch Dennis helped his grandfather clean up the dishes and square away the campsite, and then the group relaxed and the children began to play. After some time had passed one of the adults noticed the children gathered in a huddle, sneaking glances toward the group relaxing and dozing on the grass. Then the children began to spread out and approach the adult group from all sides. It seemed their plan was to sneak up on the adults and scare them. Doug and two other boys circled along the North Carolina side of the ridge while Dennis headed west on the Appalachian Trail by himself. Dennis stepped behind a bush and the adults thought he was using this as cover to make his approach.

In just a couple of minutes the "ambush" was sprung as Doug and his companions rushed into the open, yelling like demons. Dennis did not appear. Since he was the youngest, it was thought, perhaps he was just a little slower than the others. But when Dennis did not appear in two or three minutes all the members of the party began to call for him. Grandfather Clyde and father, Bill Clyde, walked out the trail in the direction Dennis had taken and the rest of the party continued to call his name, but Dennis was nowhere to be found. He has not been found to this day.

The Martins were experienced outdoorsmen, so they quickly set up a search with adults taking each of the trails that led away from their campsite. There was plenty of light since June brings the longest day of the year, although in the hollows and under the heavy tree canopy shadows would lengthen in an hour or so. One by one the searchers returned with no news. They had seen no footprints matching the shoes Dennis was wearing, and hikers they met said they had not seen a lone boy on the trail. Grandfather Clyde knew more help was needed, so he hiked back down the Bote Mountain and Anthony Creek Trails to reach the ranger station in Cades Cove. Then Clyde hiked through the now dark woods back to Spence Field. As the evening wore on a thunderstorm rolled over the mountains, deafening searchers with thunder and drenching them with cold rain.

The response by the Park Service was immediate. As Bill Clyde, Dennis's father, had been searching for his son he had met the park naturalist, Terry Chilcote. The naturalist had used his jeep to take Bill Clyde down the mountain to meet a ranger coming from the Cades Cove Ranger Station. Bill and the ranger then drove up the Bote Mountain route to within a short distance of Spence Field. The father and a ranger had thus thoroughly covered one possible route Dennis might have taken. When Dennis's grandfather reached Cades Cove, another ranger was sent up the trail leading from the west to reach Spence Field. Within a few hours of Dennis disappearing, the main trails east and west of Spence Field had been gone over by family members and by park rangers.

On the mind of the rangers was the risk hypothermia posed to Dennis. A dangerous medical condition, hypothermia occurs when the body loses heat faster than it can produce heat. A normal body temperature is about 98.6 degrees and hypothermia begins to occur when the body temperature falls below 95 degrees. Getting wet causes the body to lose heat, and if there is a wind the loss of heat is more rapid. Small people, with less body mass, will lose heat quickly. Dennis was about four feet tall and weighed fifty-five pounds. He was wearing only shorts and a T-shirt when he disappeared. During the night 2.5 inches of rain fell, and there were gusts of wind while the air temperature fell to near 50 degrees.

In addition to the danger of hypothermia, the rain presented searchers with treacherous footing on muddy trails and the loss of any footprints Dennis might have left. Dennis disappeared on Saturday, June 14. Even as they searched the trails in the Spence Field area for the first time, the Park Service was making calls to park employees and to area rescue squads asking them to assemble at the Bote Mountain trailhead early on Sunday morning. By Sunday the news of Dennis's disappearance was being broadcast over area TV stations, and that caused two problems. One was curiosity seekers who wanted to get a look at the search operations and who only made a nuisance of themselves by clogging the roads. The park superintendent reacted to this by simply closing the road into the area. The second problem was too many volunteers. Rangers found themselves swamped with offers of help from people who were not qualified or physically fit to go into the backcountry. These volunteers had to be carefully screened to make sure some of the would-be rescuers did not have to be rescued! During the day on Sunday about 250 qualified searchers were out looking for Dennis.

By Monday the story of Dennis Martin was on the national news. The Red Cross was included in the search effort to provide food for the searchers, and helicopters were brought in to transport searchers from Cades Cove to the various balds on the high crest of the mountains. Tracking dogs with their handlers were brought to the area, although continued heavy rains made slim the likelihood of finding a scent trail.

Two flashes of hope came during the week, one when a radio call from a ranger saying "the little boy has been found," was heard, but this proved to be another child who had briefly wandered away from his family. Another surge of hope occurred when a boy wearing a red T-shirt and green shorts was spotted in the Cades Cove campground. This young fellow was camping with his family and by chance had worn the same color combination of clothes as Dennis had on when he went missing.

Members of the Special Forces, also known as the Green Berets, came to assist in the search as did members of the National Guard. Billy Clyde Martin felt his son might have been kidnapped, so the FBI sent a team to assist. If a kidnapping had occurred, it had taken place on federal property. Also, Spence Field straddles the state line between Tennessee and North Carolina so there was sufficient basis for federal involvement. The national attention to the story led to psychics and clairvoyants offering their services and, in many cases, their "leads" were followed up. Not surprisingly, some of these types wanted money for their information and they were ignored. Still, numbers of well-meaning people poured into the park to help in the search with the number rising to as many as fourteen hundred on the weekend. Sadly, Friday, June 21, was Dennis's seventh birthday. By this time hope was waning that the lost boy would be found alive.

Exposure was considered the greatest danger for Dennis, but there was some concern over wild animals, especially bears and wild hogs. The mast, or nut crop, on which bears depend for much of their food, had been poor and more bears than usual were on the move looking for food. At that time there had never been a fatal bear attack in the park, but the possibility could not be ruled out. This suspicion was reinforced by the experience some of the family had with the somewhat aggressive bears during their hike into Spence Field. While no shreds of clothing had been found, orders were given that all bear feces be examined to determine if human remains were present in them. None was found.

A less likely suspect for a fatal attack was wild hogs. There is a population of wild hogs in the Smokies, dating back to the early twentieth century when Russian boars were imported to a private hunting preserve. Some of these escaped and have bred with local pigs to produce feral animals. These animals are quite destructive to flora in the park and can be dangerous to humans, although there were no known incidents, then or now, of attacks on people. An examination of hog feces showed no evidence of an attack on a human.

As an example of the thoroughness of the search, all the pit toilets at nearby backcountry campsites were examined. A ranger wearing chest-high waders was lowered into the pit of each toilet and felt with his feet to determine if a body was hidden in the vault of the toilet.

As the second week of the search began, the weather continued to be uncooperative. Frequent heavy thunderstorms drenched the mountains and on some occasions rain fell for most of the day.

Very little effective searching could be done under such circumstances. Then a report was received from Harold Key, who had been visiting the park on the day Dennis disappeared, taking photos of wildlife in the Sea Branch area. Mr. Key reported hearing a child scream and then seeing a dirty, unkempt man getting into a white car and driving away. He did not see a child. The place where Mr. Key heard and saw these things was about five miles from Spence Field. To go from the point where Dennis was last seen to Sea Branch, it would have been necessary to go for some distance across country since no trail links the two spots. From the time Dennis disappeared until the time Mr. Key saw the unkempt man did not seem long enough for anyone to cover that distance. For this reason this report was not followed up to a great extent.

On June 29 a decision was made to end the mass search for Dennis Martin. The searchers and their equipment were brought down from the mountains and the volunteers went home. After two full weeks of searching with no results, the chances of Dennis being found alive were nil. All along the searchers had been told by family members that Dennis was a shy child who probably would not call out to help them find him; he would likely respond to his name. This had made the search more difficult. Many people who get lost experience a psychological reaction that makes them afraid of people, so they hide from searchers who are very close to them. In the rhododendron and laurel thickets of the Smokies, a small person such as Dennis could hide himself from a careful searcher who was only a few feet away. However, three of the most expert trackers in the employ of the park were assigned to keep going over the area where Dennis was last seen. Arthur Whitehead, Grady Whitehead, and J. R. Buchanan would continue the hunt for the rest of the summer. No trace of Dennis was found. Clyde Martin, Dennis's grandfather, would spend weeks and days on the mountains searching for the little boy. False leads would continue to surface for another fifteen years, but none of them were productive.

The lush foliage of the Great Smoky Mountains National Park produces from one to four inches of leaf litter and debris every year. If Dennis did meet his end in the park, his remains are now buried deep in the soil of a place he and his family loved.

Dennis was gone but not forgotten. In 2009 Dennis's cousin Hayley Martin wrote about the fortieth anniversary of his disappearance. The family still grieved the loss of such a young life, and she noted that the event had forever changed the way they viewed the mountains, a place with which they have been connected for a century.

The loss of Dennis Martin's life did produce changes that have helped save other lives. The Park Service did a thorough assessment of the way in which the search was handled and, as a result, changed some of its policies to make the process more efficient. It was learned that there can be too many searchers, especially untrained ones. The current policy is to limit the number of searchers to those who have the needed skills and training. These smaller groups are more effective because they cover the ground properly and eliminate the need for repeated searches of the same area.

The large number of participants in the Dennis Martin search may have accidentally destroyed clues as to his route and whereabouts. Hundreds of people hiked the trails and woods looking for Dennis, and their very numbers may have obliterated footprints or other signs of his passing. Currently one of the first steps taken is to block off the trails leading to the point where the lost person was last seen. Hikers already on the trail are allowed to exit the area and are interviewed as to what they may have seen of the lost person, but no new hikers are allowed into the area. This preserves whatever clues there may be until the tracking dogs and expert rangers can look over the scene. A smaller number of searchers also means there is less need for logistical support to supply food and transportation. In searching, less may be more.

A good deal of study has been done into the psychology of lost persons in an effort to understand their emotions and to predict their actions. Depending on psychological factors a lost person may stay in a very limited area or they may try to cover as much distance as possible. Knowing as much as can be known about the emotional state of the lost person helps determine how large an area should be included in the initial search.

Since a lost person becomes regional news in less than twenty-four hours and national news within two days, it is now the practice to appoint one person to deal with the press. In addition to the simple news that someone is lost, the park works to let the public know what they can do to help, such as keeping an eye out for anyone fitting the description or matching a photograph of the lost person, and what they need to avoid in order not to hinder the search, for example, staying out of the area and not getting in the way.

Technological advances have made search efforts more effective. Helicopters are much improved over the models used in 1969 and more of them are available for use in search missions. The dense tree cover of most of the Smokies means that searches from the air are not particularly effective, but during the seasons when leaves are on the trees helicopters can transport search teams and supplies into remote areas of the park quickly, saving hours if not days of travel by foot or horseback.

The advent of small, lightweight Global Positioning System (GPS) devices makes it much easier for the person coordinating a search to know precisely where search teams have been and where they still need to go. An increasing number of hikers carry a variation of the GPS device, which they can turn on if they become lost to broadcast their precise location to aircraft flying over the area.

The tragic disappearance of Dennis Martin continues to affect the lives of those who knew and loved him. But the lessons learned from the search for him have been true life-savers for others. To this extent, the sad events surrounding Dennis have not been in vain.

Simple Lessons for Parents with Young Children

Keep the group close together. It doesn't take long for a child to get lost.

Impress on children that if they get lost they should sit down and stay in that place.

Tell children that rangers are like policemen; it is all right to talk to them.

Put a lanyard with a whistle around the neck of each child. A person can blow a whistle longer than they can shout and nothing in nature sounds like a whistle.

CHAPTER 6

You Can't Fight Mother Nature
and Win

It looked like good weather for an overnight hike on the Appalachian Trail in the Great Smoky Mountains. It was cold and there were several inches of snow on the ground at the higher elevations, but these were just the sort of challenges teenage boys like, especially when they have been Boy Scouts for several years and have learned something about the outdoors. The hike would not be too long or too challenging. Eugene Smith, who led Troop 95 from nearby Morristown, Tennessee, had with him only three boys—Lee Smith, Geoff Hague, and Steve Wolfe—and two other adults: assistant troop leader Marvin Horner and Rev. Pitser Lyons. The destination of the group was the Icewater Springs Shelter, three miles out the Appalachian Trail from the parking lot at Newfound Gap.

The group reached the trailhead at Newfound Gap at a reasonable hour in the morning of February 7, 1970, and hiked the relatively easy trail three miles to reach Icewater Springs. They gained about a thousand feet in elevation from

Newfound Gap to Mount Ambler and then descended a couple of feet to reach the shelter at the springs. When the group reached the shelter, they set up their camp and Marvin Horner and Reverend Lyons returned to their car at Newfound Gap; the next day would be Sunday and Lyons had to conduct services at his church.

When camp was set up the boys began to do what one would expect boys to do with snow on the ground; they began to throw snowballs at each other. And, as will happen with teenage males, the play became a little rough, so Troop Leader Smith called his charges into camp to begin preparing supper.

Geoff had recently completed the requirements for earning his Explorer badge, and he had become fascinated with the topic of wilderness survival. He had just watched a TV program on the subject and he and the other boys had talked about the program on the hike out to Icewater Springs. Now, it seemed, Geoff wanted to try out his newly acquired skills by building his own fire. Wood was gathered but, with snow having been on the ground for several days, all the fuel was damp and the fire would not kindle. Geoff kept working at the self-imposed task, getting down on the ground to blow on the fire, getting his clothes pretty wet in the process.

Wet clothes can be endured while a person is active, but it is not easy to sleep in them. The wet cloth evaporates heat from the body so that a person wearing wet clothes never gets really warm and can't sleep. Mr. Smith knew this so he insisted that Geoff put on dry clothes before getting into his sleeping bag for the night.

Morning brought temperatures in the teens and heavy skies, but the agenda for the campers called for having breakfast and then hiking the three miles back to their vehicle. Breakfast was finished before 9:00 a.m. and the group made ready to leave. Lee Smith was told to stay behind a few minutes to finish tidying up the campsite and to catch up as soon as he could. Steve Wolfe took the lead, Geoff was in the middle of the line, and Troop Leader Smith came last so he could keep an eye on the hikers.

The group made the ascent from Icewater Springs to the junction of the Appalachian Trail with the Boulevard Trail. Boulevard would have gone to their right and would lead a hiker to the top of Mount LeConte five miles away. The names, direction, and mileage to destinations are all clearly posted at the junction of the trails. When the group reached the trail junction, they took a short rest after their uphill climb and then got ready to start along the Appalachian Trail for Newfound Gap. Geoff was not ready to go, even when his fellow scout, Steve, urged him to do so. As it was later remembered, Geoff said he would stay where he was and wait for Lee Smith and would hike out with him. Given this assurance Mr. Smith and Steve Wolfe left for the Gap.

Mr. Smith and Steve did not have long to wait at Newfound Gap before Lee showed up—alone. He had not seen Geoff at any point along the way. The three then made the hike back to Icewater Springs looking for their missing partner, but they had no success. The shelter at the Springs is a little off the trail, so they went farther east to a rocky outcrop called Charlies Bunion thinking that Geoff might have gone back toward the shelter to meet Lee but missed the turn to the campsite and continued along the trail. Still no sign of Geoff. Returning to the junction of the Appalachian Trail and the Boulevard Trail, they went some distance toward Mount LeConte, just in case Geoff had walked off without looking at the trail signs. No luck.

It was pretty clear to all three that Geoff was lost and the best thing for them to do was get help to look for him. They hiked back to their car and drove to park headquarters at Sugarlands Visitors Center just outside Gatlinburg. They were worried, but there a few comforting factors: Geoff knew at least the basics of how to survive in the woods, he was warmly dressed in a corduroy coat and sweatshirt as well as heavy twill Scout pants and boots, he had a good sleeping bag, and he had his pack containing food and matches. The situation was serious but not desperate. The greatest challenge was the weather. Snow had fallen lightly for much of the day, becoming heavier as night fell, and another six inches had accumulated at Newfound Gap, which meant there would be some deeper drifts in places along the trails. By the time the report was received at park headquarters, the daylight was fading fast.

The Park Service used the hours of darkness to get ready for a thorough search on Monday morning. Seven teams of searchers, including Mr. Smith, were assigned routes that would cover from end to end all the trails connected to the route the Scout group had originally followed.

Snow continued to fall most of the day on Monday, but the trail searchers were all able to cover their assigned routes. They found nothing. It was beginning to look as if Geoff had gone off the trail. The Civil Air Patrol and the Rescue Service at an air base in Georgia had been alerted, but there was nothing they could do until the weather cleared.

By Tuesday over 130 people were out looking for Geoff, but the weather was brutal with temperatures in the teens and wind speeds up to 25 miles per hour, which produced a terrific wind-chill factor. Only on Tuesday afternoon did the wind abate enough to allow helicopters to begin lifting searchers and supplies to the higher peaks of the Smokies. The third day of searching on Wednesday saw double the numbers out in the woods but brought no better news.

Specially trained dogs were brought in to help with the search. Some search dogs need a trail left on solid objects such as the ground or rocks, but others are called "air-scent" dogs. They pick up the scent from air that has been in contact with anything the lost person has touched. The snow would hamper ground tracker dogs, but the air-scent animals would have a better chance of tracking Geoff. Evangelist Billy Graham sent two of these dogs, which were taken on the hunt by Graham's son, Franklin Graham. These dog teams were deployed on Friday, the fifth day of all-out searching, and they found scattered indications of Geoff's presence along the Boulevard Trail in the direction of Mount LeConte. This encouraged the searchers to request more dog teams, and canine help began to arrive from as far away as Washington State. The weekend also brought moderating temperatures and more than 350 people to assist in the search. Still Geoff was nowhere to be found.

Monday, February 16, brought a discouraging find. On a rock in the middle of Walker Camp Prong, searchers found a pack containing clothes, food, and other supplies. Family members identified the items as belonging to Geoffrey. Wherever he was, Geoff now did not have the items necessary for survival. Now the search would concentrate on the drainage area of the creek where Geoff's possessions had been found. This would not be an easy task since the Walker Camp Prong contains some of the steepest slopes and thickest rhododendron thickets in the entire park. The second day of searching in this area led to the discovery of Geoff's body.

When found, the warmest clothes Geoff had with him were scattered around him as he lay at the base of a tree. His body was still almost completely covered by snow. A medical examination led to the conclusion that he had died on Sunday, February 8 or early on the 9th, only a few hours after he had gone missing from his hiking companions. The removal of clothes is often observed in victims of hypothermia, since the victims of the condition think they are too hot. How Geoff came to go toward Mount LeConte along the Boulevard Trail instead of following the Appalachian Trail to Newfound Gap or why he left the trail to bushwhack along a stream will never be known. What is known is you cannot win a fight with Mother Nature. A few days after Geoff's death J. Clark Rhodes wrote "A Meditation on the Great Smoky Mountains" in memory of Geoffrey Burns Hague.

As recently as 2012 people were still losing their challenge to Mother Nature in the Great Smokies. Derek Leuking lived in Louisville, Tennessee, a small town not far from the Great Smoky Mountains National Park. At age twenty-four he was seemingly happy with his life, having graduated from Johnson University in Knoxville, and was employed at the Peninsula Behavioral Health Center.

On March 14, 2012, he left home but did not go to work; instead he headed for the mountains. He spent one night in Gatlinburg, one night at the Smokemont Campground in the park, and a third night at a motel in Cherokee, North Carolina. During this time he had visited several outdoors sporting goods stores and had purchased quite a bit of camping material. This was a little unusual since Derek liked to go for day hikes but had never gotten involved in backpacking, nor was he in the physical condition backpacking demands. He was not lean and fit.

But if Derek was not a backpacker in the real sense, he did like the virtual version of the activity. Derek was a loyal fan of the TV reality program *Man vs. Wild* and enjoyed both watching the show and talking about it. Did he decide to try to survive the wilderness for real?

A surveillance camera in the motel where he stayed in Cherokee, North Carolina, showed him leaving his room at about 4:00 a.m. on March 17 with a small daypack. By this time Derek's family was looking for him because his supervisor at work had called to ask why he had not reported for duty. Online credit card records told them that he was in Cherokee, so they drove there but arrived after he had left. As luck would have it, as the family drove back toward Tennessee they spotted Derek's white Ford Escape parked at Newfound Gap. They also found in the vehicle his wallet, the keys to the car, and a note saying "Don't look for me." But, of course, they did look for him.

Only one trail passes through Newfound Gap, the Appalachian Trail, but the parking area is a favorite point for visitors. The panoramic views with mile upon mile of mountain range rolling away into the distance cause almost every car driving along the Trans-Mountain Road from Cherokee, North Carolina, to Gatlinburg, Tennessee, to stop for a leg-stretcher and a photo. The weather had been good on the day Derek left his car there and hundreds of people had been in the lot. But no one had seen him. Perhaps he had arrived very early, having left Cherokee at 4:00 a.m. for a drive of forty-five minutes or less.

The paucity of available routes out of the Gap encouraged park officials as they began their search in response to the report filed by Derek's family. A quick search was made along the Appalachian Trail in both directions from Newfound Gap and, when Derek was not found, search teams were sent down the connecting trails. The operative word here is "down." The Appalachian Trail at this point runs along the high crest of the Smokies, and trails branching off from it go down into Tennessee in one direction and North Carolina in the other. The farther from Newfound Gap one goes the more trails are passed, so soon search teams were looking in most of the park. Searchers covered more than fifty miles of trails during the first two days of the mission.

Over the years the Park Service has learned that a small number of trained searchers is better than a large crowd of untrained volunteers, so the number of people out on the trail was kept to dozens rather than hundreds. All hikers coming into the search area were shown a picture of Derek, but none of them had passed him. A park official was tasked to serve as a public relations contact and make sure news and pictures of Derek went out to all area media outlets.

Helicopters flew over the woods since the trees had not yet put out leaves and visibility was good, and the Civil Air Patrol participated in the search. Dog teams were brought in, but there were occasional heavy showers and no scent trail was ever found.

For Derek's family this was a very trying time. They were, however, given an important job to allow them to aid in the search; they were stationed in the parking area at Newfound Gap with photos of Derek and were encouraged to talk to as many people as they could to help spread the word. One of the family members started a Facebook page titled "Find Derek Leuking."

After a week of hard searching the Park Service had no clues, no leads at all as to where to continue to look. As the search wound down one technique was to begin to explore places along the trail where the woods looked open and it would be appealing to go off the trail. In the Smokies such open spaces don't last long, and a hiker going off the established path may soon find himself in a jungle-like tangle. This means searchers can only look at a relatively small part of the entire land surface; some of the terrain is too heavily covered in bushes or too steep to be readily traversed. This same heavy cover of vegetation muffles sound, so a cry for help can be heard only for a short distance.

With no clues the Park Service reluctantly scaled down the search for Derek. His family did make one last attempt, rallying sixty people to walk some of the trails one more time and handing out over three thousand flyers asking for information about Derek. The park officials continued to collect leads about Derek and follow up on each one of them.

—◦—

The disappearance of Derek Leuking led authorities to uncover a larger mystery. While searching for Derek on Tuesday, March 20, a ranger noticed an automobile parked about one mile south of the Sugarlands Visitors Center at a "quiet walkway." Scattered along the roads in the park are pull-overs where visitors may leave their vehicles to take an easy walk into the forest. These quiet walkways are short, only a few hundred yards in length at most, they are well graded, and some of them are paved to allow visitors with physical challenges to get off the road and have at least a taste of the quietness and grandeur of nature. The automobile was still in the same spot two days later. While it is not unusual for a vehicle to be parked at a trailhead for several days, this quiet walkway did not connect with the park's trail system. It was a closed loop leading to the banks of the West Prong of the Little Pigeon River. There was no reason a car should be parked there for such a long time. A walk of only a few minutes revealed that the owner of the car was not on the walkway, nor was he on the banks of the river. A check of the license plates showed that the vehicle belonged to Michael Giovanni Cocchini and gave the authorities a phone number for his parents.

Michael, age twenty-three, had moved to the Gatlinburg area from Nashville about seven weeks earlier to begin a job in a retail establishment. He had made a few new friends and, on Sunday, March 18, had gone with a group of them to a "big box" store in Sevierville. At about 2:00 p.m. he left his friends and, apparently, drove to the park and left his car at the quiet walkway. Once it was determined who the missing person was, and how long his vehicle had been empty, a search was mounted for Michael.

Searchers on foot and a dog team followed the short walkway and then fanned out into the woods. The banks of the river got close attention simply because the water is an attractive feature and people are drawn to it, but a search both up and down the stream found no clues about Michael. After a week, just about the time the search for Derek was scaling down, the attempt to find Michael was eased up. By that time a note had been found in the room where he lived that said "Thanks for everything." Although the conclusion might be drawn that this was a suicide note, the investigation into the death did not conclude that this was the case.

The double failure to find missing persons was depressing to the men and women of the Park Service and the trained volunteer groups who had participated in the effort. Most "lost" people in the Smokies are simply people who have gotten separated from their group and they are found rather quickly. Of those who are genuinely lost, about 90 percent are found in a few days, either discovered by search parties or by walking out of the woods on their own. When dozens of dedicated people have expended the tremendous physical and emotional energy demanded by a search, coming up empty is truly depressing. The end of a search is also devastating for the families involved, but when there are no clues to follow, the Park Service must face making a hard decision.

There is no set time limit for how long a search will continue, but there must be leads to follow for there to be any reasonable hope in continuing a search.

In August 2012, a park employee working near the quiet walkway where Michael had disappeared found a backpack that was identified as belonging to the missing man. An intensive search unearthed shreds of clothing matching the clothes Michael was wearing when last seen. Then his cellphone was found and, nearby, fragments of a human skull. The Regional Forensic Center in Knoxville identified these as belonging to Michael. These pitiful remains were found within five hundred yards of the quiet walkway, a testimony to the density of the foliage in the park.

⌐▬◡▬⌐

As of 2015 no solution has been found for the disappearance of Derek Leuking. His family still misses him.

With ten million people visiting the Great Smoky Mountains National Park, one would think that getting lost in a crowd of people going to the restroom or looking for a soft drink machine would be the likely thing to happen. With so many people visiting, how wild can the park be? The answer is quite wild, indeed. Most of the visitors limit their activities to sites accessible by road, driving the Trans-Mountain Road from Gatlinburg to Cherokee, visiting Clingmans Dome, and taking the loop road through Cades Cove. There are some popular trails that are crowded such as the Abrams Falls Trail or the Alum Cave Bluffs Trail, but there are miles of lightly used trails that lead into genuine wilderness areas. Off these trails the challenges of terrain and foliage are such that even strong people can exhaust themselves. The Great Smokies is a place to enjoy; it is not a place where one should abandon common sense and challenge Mother Nature. You can't fight Mother Nature and win.

CHAPTER 7

Common Sense Saves Lives

ERIC JOHNSON AND RANDY LAWS OF JOHNSON CITY, Tennessee, were wise beyond their years, and they had good training about how to live in the outdoors. Both boys were fifteen years old in the autumn of 1974 and both were Eagle Scouts. As a special adventure they convinced their parents to let them undertake a hike along the Appalachian Trail from Friday to Sunday following Thanksgiving. Because of their experience in camping and because both were level-headed young men, their parents agreed.

Because they had already hiked most of the Appalachian Trail in the area, they decided to tackle one section they had not yet done. They would enter the park at its eastern end at Davenport Gap and follow the AT to Newfound Gap on the Trans-Mountain Road from Gatlinburg to Cherokee.

Henry and Wanneta Johnson drove the boys to the park on the day after Thanksgiving and waited while the pair picked up their backcountry permits. The weather was cold but the skies were clear when their parents dropped them off at Davenport Gap, though some snow would normally be expected at the higher altitudes in the park. The trail is steadily uphill as it climbs toward the high crest of the Smokies, but the two fit young men made good time. When they stopped for lunch, they saw their first sign of change; the sky had become overcast. Keeping up a steady pace, they passed Mount Guyot just as snow began to fall and, by the time they reached their destination for the first night at the shelter at Tricorner Knob, snow was falling fast.

A long hike, full stomachs, and warm sleeping bags gave them a sound sleep all Friday night, but daylight on Saturday brought a surprise. Snow was falling heavily, the wind was high, and there were drifts several feet deep. By the end of the day on Saturday, the snow was eighteen inches deep. Eric and Randy faced a decision with potential life-and-death consequences: Should they try to continue their hike to the next shelter and then go on to Newfound Gap, or should they stay where they were, conserving their food and shelter until help came to them?

They made a brief attempt to continue their hike, but the snow was so deep that progress was reduced to a crawl and the trail was completely obliterated. They followed the course of good sense. The two Eagle Scouts returned to the shelter at Tricorner Knob, got their supplies under cover in the shelter, and stamped out the letters H E L P in letters twenty feet tall in an open space near the shelter. Then they concentrated on staying dry and as warm as possible, the key to survival. Wet clothes wick heat away from the body and exposure to wind speeds up the process. Having done all they could, the young men sat down to wait.

In Johnson City the news about the unexpected snow-storm caused the parents some concern, but the weather reports did not say just how deep the snow was at the upper elevations of the park. On Sunday afternoon, as scheduled, Henry and Wanneta Johnson drove to Gatlinburg and, to their shock, found the road through the park to Newfound Gap closed because of the heavy snow. At Sugarlands Visitors Center, the park headquarters, the Johnsons described their plight to park officials, who provided a ranger and a four-wheel drive vehicle to help them reach the pickup point for the hikers. No hikers were at the Gap and, as darkness fell, it became obvious that they needed to return to park headquarters so a search and rescue mission could be planned.

On Monday morning searchers using snowmobiles were sent from the Cosby area of the park to search the Appalachian Trail from east to west, and teams on foot were sent in from Newfound Gap to search west to east. The snow was so deep and so powdery that the combination of snow and rugged terrain stopped the snowmobiles in their tracks. The machines could not gain traction to move uphill. At Newfound Gap the snow depth and the high wind velocity made it almost impossible for search teams to move on foot. The team on snowshoes took nine hours to reach Icewater Springs Shelter, just over three miles from their starting point.

Truly foul weather in November in Tennessee is usually of short duration, and this was the case in this search. Tuesday dawned bright and clear and a helicopter from the University of Tennessee in Knoxville took off to fly over the route of the Appalachian Trail. In the helicopter were Dr. Robert Lash, the founder of the Lifestar medical evacuation program for the university's medical school, and Ranger Bud Inman. At Tricorner Knob, Eric was confident that the clear weather would bring an air search. To help the searchers spot their position, they put a red backpack on the ground near the H E L P sign they had stamped out. The helicopter spotted the stranded hikers and circled over them to let them know help was on the way.

That help was in the form of a Chinook helicopter equipped with a hoist cable and carrying nurses. There were some winds along the high peaks and the ride was not smooth, nor was it easy for the pilot to keep the machine steady over the pickup zone, but a cable with a harness was lowered to the boys.

In the shelter the hikers were jubilant that their ordeal was over, but they had to decide who would ascend first. They settled the matter in a time-honored fashion; they flipped a coin. Randy won but soon Eric joined him in the helicopter. Eric later recalled being hoisted out of the Tricorner Knob Shelter as "the scariest part of the entire experience."

A quick examination showed the young men to be in good condition with only some slight dehydration and Eric suffering minor frostbite on his toes. They spent a few days in the hospital in Johnson City and then returned to classes at their high school.

The following year, on December 3, 1975, the first anniversary of the rescue of her son, Wanneta Johnson showed up at park headquarters with the biggest, prettiest poinsettia she could find. She was still making her annual pilgrimage in 2014. She says the rangers are angels on earth; to her they are all ten feet tall. She never lost faith the rangers would find her son, although she says her husband was somewhat despondent by the time they were found. Mrs. Johnson says she has instructed Eric to continue delivering a poinsettia every December 3 after she is gone.

Eric lost contact with Randy after high school, but Eric went on to have a career in the FBI and as a special agent with the Drug Enforcement Agency. In 2009, the thirty-fifth anniversary of his rescue, Eric joined his mother in the annual visit to the park and presented the staff with a plaque of appreciation. Although all those who participated in the rescue are no longer at the park, the gratitude of the Johnson family goes on. There is also gratitude for the good sense the two Eagle Scouts showed during their ordeal.

Staying on the trails is one of the best common sense rules anyone can apply. If there were no trails it would be impossible to penetrate most of the park, because anyone attempting to go cross-country would soon confront an almost impenetrable tangle of foliage. Rhododendron, mountain laurel, dog hobble, and thousands of other varieties of plants become so thick and intertwined that passage through them is impossible. Getting into such a tangle puts a person in a condition that is claustrophobic, confining, and confusing. The story of Cindy Lee Webster illustrates that point.

Cindy Lee Webster, age twenty-six, taught outdoor education in Bloomington, Indiana. She was skilled in map and compass reading and wanted to teach those skills to her students. On the afternoon of Friday, March 22, 1974, she checked in at the Greenbrier Ranger Station to get back-country permits for three days. She said she intended to spend the first night at the Porters Creek Shelter, then go cross-country to the Appalachian Trail (no trail connects the Porters Creek Shelter with the Appalachian Trail) and spend her second night at Icewater Springs Shelter. On her third day she would hike to Mount LeConte for her third night and then would come down LeConte via the Rainbow Falls Trail and return to Greenbrier via the Grapeyard Ridge Trail. This was a strenuous route and would involve covering a good number of miles each day to meet the schedule. But, Ms Webster had promised to be back in Bloomington for her birthday celebration on March 26.

Cindy hiked in to the Porters Creek Shelter on Saturday and shared the site with some other campers. The weather was good on Saturday, but Sunday morning brought overcast skies and a hint of snow. Still, the Icewater Springs Shelter was not much more than two miles away, if one could go as the crow flies—which one cannot. A quick look at a topographic map shows the contour lines are very close together along the route Cindy had chosen, meaning the slope would be very steep. But the immediate prospect was one of open woods, so Cindy took a compass bearing that would bring her to the Appalachian Trail at an appropriate point and set off.

Then everything began to go wrong, snow began to fall, the foliage became more tangled, progress became slower, and Cindy began getting wet. Calling on her experience, she knew she had to find shelter and get dry and warm again. Finally, she reached the top of a ridge, which one she did not know since she had lost her map. There was enough flat space to pitch her tent, a small backpackers model, and the tent would be visible to any search from the air. Cindy also put a spare parka and a brightly colored backpack in some small trees to further mark her location. Then she got inside the tent and had some food. Again, a good common sense decision had been made that would save a life.

The weather continued to be such that air searches were not feasible; fog, rain, and snow shrouded the high peaks where Cindy Webster was thought to be. If modern technology could not do the job, the Park Service had an old-fashioned substitute in reserve: man tracking. One of the legendary figures in the lore of the Great Smoky Mountains National Park is now retired ranger Dwight McCarter. Dwight is a native of the area, a descendant of one of the first families to settle in the Gatlinburg area. Dwight finished high school and then served in the US Army before taking a job with the Park Service. He performed a variety of jobs before becoming a backcountry ranger and, along the way, learned the skills of man tracking from "old timers" in both the Park Service and in the area. He also developed the strength and stamina to walk the mountains. A few years after the Webster incident in September 1978 he would begin a hike at Fontana Dam and end at the Cosby Campground fourteen hours later, covering about seventy miles at an average speed of almost six and one-half miles per hour, a rate equal to the speed of a good jogger on flat ground.

Following a quick search along the trails in the Porters Flat area where Cindy was last seen, Dwight was assigned to try to find marks of her passage if she had gone off trail. On Tuesday, March 28, he did so. Cindy's tracks led up steep slopes and through tangled vegetation, and Dwight was making even slower progress than Cindy had since he had to keep looking for small signs of her passage such as broken twigs, scuffed leaves, and an occasional partial footprint in the snow that had managed to stick to the steep slopes. A helicopter flew over late in the afternoon as the weather began to clear and, much to Dwight's joy, it later flew back over his position and then flew in a straight line and began to circle a point on the ridge ahead. The position being circled was a continuation of the route he had been following for hours. The tracker was not the first to spot the lost person, but he had pointed the way the air searchers should go.

Food, water, and medical supplies were dropped to Cindy as Dwight and other foot searchers began to close in on her location, but when they arrived they found she was in quite good condition.

Cindy Webster was able to walk out of the woods on her own power, arriving at a trailhead about midnight. A few hours later she was reunited with her family, a reunion she might not have experienced had she not made a good common sense decision.

﹘﹖

On rare occasions good luck is a substitute for good common sense. Chad Hunter, age twenty-three, was a student at the University of Tennessee in Knoxville. His home was in Memphis and spring break was approaching, so he decided on an adventure all on his own. He worked out a route for a four-day hike in the Great Smoky Mountains National Park that would utilize mostly trails but would also involve some bushwhacking cross-country. The area he chose was in the Greenbrier section of the park, the same area where Cindy

Lee Webster had found herself in difficulty. Hunter planned to begin his hike on Monday, March 14, 2011, and to complete it on Thursday, and he arranged to call his parents when he got back to a telephone on Thursday.

As Chad took to the trail on Monday, the weather was rainy but not unseasonably cold. He walked up the Grapeyard Ridge Trail to Campsite #32 on Injun Creek. The name of the creek is not a disrespectful reference to the Native Americans who once inhabited the area but is a corruption of "engine." During the time when the area was owned by logging companies, a steam engine toppled into the creek and its remains may still be seen there.

On Tuesday, Chad had a long and difficult day scheduled for himself. He would follow the Grapeyard Trail to its intersection with the Ramsay Cascade road, follow that until it became a foot trail, and continue to Ramsay Cascade, an attractive waterfall. At that point he planned to leave the trail and navigate through some of the steepest and most dense terrain in the park to reach the Appalachian Trail in the vicinity of Mount Guyot.

The trail walk from Campsite #32 to Ramsay Cascade was not overly difficult because trail crews had installed stone steps and footbridges. But when Chad reached the end of the trail at Ramsay Cascade, the story changed quickly. He followed the course of Ramsay Prong, the stream that creates the cascade, but found the going to be very steep with large boulders and huge logs often blocking his path. At this point, about a half-mile above the end of the trail, he decided to go toward the ridgeline. Fighting through the tangles of rhododendron and other low-growing vegetation soon left

Chad confused and unsure of his proper route. At nightfall he found a spot to put up his tent, prepared some food, and tried to sleep.

Wednesday was worse. The thicket had become so dense that Chad spent six to seven hours covering about one-half mile. During this struggle with the bushes, Chad made the decision to abandon his pack because it kept snagging on limbs. This meant his sleeping bag and most of his food were left behind and there was no water to be found on the steep ridge. With only the clothes he was wearing and a small fanny pack, Chad struggled on until he reached a relatively flat and somewhat open area. If abandoning his pack was a bad idea, staying still and waiting for rescue was a better one. The problem was, no one knew he was lost. Chad was not supposed to phone his parents until Thursday evening.

With little food or water Chad stayed where he was from sometime late Wednesday afternoon until Sunday morning. By that time he was completely out of food and the few scraps of snow he had been able to find in sheltered places had all melted so he had no water either. Now Chad made his second good decision. Normally, walking down-hill is easier and will usually lead one to water and, eventually, to other people; but Chad knew the Appalachian Trail was somewhere up there on the high crest. Knowing the difficulties of going through the thickets below him, Chad decided to go up. On the spur of Mount Guyot, he struck the trail and followed it to the shelter at Tricorner Knob. About 7:00 p.m. on Sunday, Chad, to his immense joy, saw not only the shelter but four hikers cooking their suppers. How good the food smelled! Chad had eaten three grubs, a worm, and some fern heads and nothing else for the last several hours.

It is customary for those hiking the Appalachian Trail from end to end to adopt trail names for use during their trip. In the Tricorner Knob Shelter were "Hap" (Mike Meadows) and "Pa Bert," both recent retirees. "Johnny Appleseed" (Nate Provost) and "Mango" (James McCullum) were recent high school graduates who were hiking the trail as an adventure before getting on with their lives.

Just as the two groups of hikers were finishing their meals, they heard a voice from outside the shelter: "Hello? I need help." When the hikers had arrived at the shelter, they had found a note in the log book which is kept at each such facility. A ranger had written that a hiker was lost and that everyone passing through the area should be on the alert for him. When they heard a plea for help, they knew exactly who it was.

None of the four had any medical training, but they knew the signs of hypothermia and dehydration so they swung into action. Preparation was started on a meal, Chad was given water, and he was wrapped in sleeping bags to get warm. Then the group did what any self-respecting person does in the twenty-first century; they got out their cellphones. There was no signal at the shelter, so two of them walked to the top of a nearby peak and got a weak signal and called 911. The emergency dispatcher gave them the number of the nearest ranger station, but their signal faded out before they were able to place the call. They wandered around about twenty minutes before they found another weak signal; they were able to contact the ranger station at Cosby and then help was on the way.

At 2:30 a.m. a ranger and two paramedics arrived at Tricorner Knob Shelter. Chad was given fluids via an IV and scrapes and lacerations were bandaged. Chad was in no condition to walk out on his own, and the distance to the nearest road was such that a large number of people would have been required to carry him that distance, so the decision was made to evacuate him by air.

Daylight brought gusting winds and the only available landing zone for a helicopter was rather small. The Park Service helicopter was not suited for making the evacuation under these conditions, so the Tennessee Highway Patrol sent one of their hoist-equipped helicopters. A stretcher was lowered and Chad was soon on his way to a local hospital where his parents were waiting. His injuries required only a few days of recovery.

Chad's case is a classic example of underestimating the challenges of hiking off trail while overestimating one's ability to travel cross-country. It also illustrates the importance of keeping available food supplies with you and not abandoning any gear that might provide shelter. Chad Hunter made some poor decisions, but in the end, common sense saved his life.

All the accounts in this chapter have involved Tricorner Knob. There is nothing sinister about the location, but it is in a remote area of the park. The elevation of Tricorner Knob is 6,120 feet, making it one of the higher peaks in the Smoky range. The mountain is not only remote, it is part of an area with a dense spruce-fir forest, and it has been largely untouched by human history. The Cherokee who lived in the area did not visit the high country often because it was not a good hunting ground. Arnold Guyot measured the elevation of Tricorner Knob during his exploring expedition in 1859, but it was not until the Appalachian Trail was constructed through the area in 1935 that many people came to the area. The shelter at the Knob holds twelve and has a water source.

Two of the accounts in this chapter have illustrated the danger and difficulty of hiking off the established trails. A primary common sense rule is "Stay on the trail."

CHAPTER 8

If You Go In Together,
Come Out Together

ONE OF THE BASIC SAFETY RULES IN THE OUTDOORS IS "keep your group together." This does not mean there must be a tightly spaced line of hikers going along the trail in march step. It does mean someone leads the line and no one passes the leader; someone is "tail-end Charlie" and no one gets behind Charlie. Within those limits people can go at their own pace and enjoy what appeals to them. Certainly, the members of a group should know where the others are, in a general sense, and there should be regular times when the group comes together to make sure everyone is present. This basic rule will help ensure that if you go in together you will come out together, all present and in good order.

When a group disintegrates, trouble can arise in a hurry. That is precisely what happened to Mark Hanson from Newport, Kentucky; and Ben Fish and John Chidester, both from Prestonburg, Kentucky. All three were students from Eastern Kentucky State University who came to the Great Smoky Mountains to spend their spring break in March 1975. Their plan was to pick up the Appalachian Trail at the Big Creek Ranger Station at the east end of the park and hike about sixteen miles to the Tricorner Knob Shelter. This route would make it necessary to climb about forty-six hundred feet over the course of their hike.

The weather the first week of March in 1975 had been terrible, as early March often is in the mountains. The unsettled weather accompanying the change of seasons can be exaggerated by the wind flow over the high peaks, producing snow at high altitudes and flooding rains at lower elevations. The change of seasons is also a prime time for tornadoes in the area. All these weather conditions had occurred in the Smoky Mountains in the days preceding the planned trip, but the three young men ignored the weather forecast and continued with their plans, hitting the trail on March 9.

Unfortunately, the students were not properly equipped for the hike. They did not have adequate waterproof jackets and were not wearing wool shirts and pants; instead they wore the same clothes they wore to class at the university—cotton jeans, sweaters, and sweatshirts. Cotton is a very comfortable cloth in hot weather, but it does not have the ability to block the wind and, worse, it absorbs water. Wool sheds water for a time and, even when it becomes wet, will still retain a large degree of body heat. The boys undoubtedly wished they had warm waterproof clothes almost immediately after leaving the trailhead, because it began to snow quite heavily and a strong wind howled down the trail. Between Low Gap and the Cosby Knob trail shelter John Chidester had had enough. His boots were not waterproof, and his feet were wet and freezing cold. He made a decision that may have saved his life. John turned back to the car and drove away to find a place to spend the night.

Back on the trail Mark and Ben were facing an increasingly daunting task. They were still toiling uphill, still battling the wind and snow, and daylight was running out. They had reached Camel Gap but that was only halfway to their goal of Tricorner Knob. They were much closer to Cosby Knob and the shelter there than they were to Tricorner, but having passed Cosby Knob, they did not want to turn back and give up their hard-earned distance on the trail, so they continued on their way.

By this point, Mark and Ben felt their energy was exhausted. Although they thought of themselves as physically fit, the mountains require more stamina than they, or most people, imagine. Running on a track or treadmill, lifting weights, and doing yoga does not really prepare a person for a strenuous hike up one of the mountain trails. Also, sixteen miles may not sound like a long distance when sitting in a comfortable chair, but most people cannot walk nearly that far, especially on their first day on the trail. It takes months of conditioning and days of hiking before one should consider a sixteen-mile uphill hike, and if the weather is filthy, even the best-conditioned hiker should take a day off.

Not long after passing Camel Gap, Mark began to show signs of hypothermia. He declared his pack was too heavy and that he didn't need it, so he dropped it on the trail. Ben did not have the strength remaining to convince his friend to keep his pack with him, even though the contents of the pack were Mark's only hope of survival. Somehow, the pair reached Mount Guyot and the shelter at Tricorner Knob was within reach, only the light was fading and the trail was obliterated by snow. Still they slogged on for some time. If they had been able to see, Mark would have known that he had only a quarter of a mile to go to reach the shelter, but, in the darkness, he ran out of energy and out of hope. He sat down and said he would go no farther. Ben, not in good shape himself, went on ahead, hoping to find help, but after only a couple hundred yards he collapsed on the trail. With his last strength he unrolled his sleeping bag and crawled inside. That act saved his life.

When light became strong enough to see the trail the next morning, Ben looked for Mark but he did not see any signs of him, so he decided to press on to Tricorner Knob Shelter, which he reached in a few minutes—he had been only a couple of hundred yards away when he stopped the night before. There were other backpackers in the shelter, and they helped Ben make it out to the Cosby area of the park where he reported Mark missing. A ranger on duty at Cosby used an all-terrain vehicle (ATV) to take Ben back to the place where he thought he had become separated from his friend, but nothing else could be done that day because of falling darkness. A full search was undertaken the following day, but it was hampered seriously by heavy rainfall. Mark Hanson's body was found on March 17, off the trail by about two miles, along the banks of Buck Fork Creek. Apparently, after Ben had gone ahead, Mark made another attempt to move on. He seemed to have started downhill and entered the drainage of Buck Fork, then kept going until he was overcome by hypothermia.

Hindsight always makes events clearer, but some important lessons are offered by this tragedy. Hiking in cold, wet weather takes special equipment and is not much fun. If the forecast is poor, hikers should reschedule their departure date. If things seem too tough, don't be ashamed to turn back. John Chidester made that decision, and it would have been appropriate for the entire group to have talked over the matter and stuck together. Even if one person was allowed to go back alone, the remaining two needed to stick together. When Mark first stopped in the trail and discarded his pack, a good decision would have been for both young men to help each other get into their sleeping bags. This would have likely led to the survival of both. If you go in together, come out together.

The outcome was less tragic, but the same lesson applies to a case ten years later involving Walt Johnson of Greenwood, Indiana, and Rick Callahan of Indianapolis. They were both college students and wanted a break from their studies at the end of the academic year. Knowing from experience that it takes time to get all the muscles going for hiking, the pair planned a trip that would give them time to acclimate to the trail. They planned to hike from Cades Cove to Spence Field, following the Anthony Creek Trail to its junction with the Appalachian Trail and Spence Field. The field is a large, grassy area popular with hikers that has a good water supply near the end of the trail. This would be a rather easy first day, since the distance to be covered was about five miles and did not contain too many steep sections. The second day of the trip was to follow the Appalachian Trail east to Derrick Knob, a distance of about six miles that involved crossing over Thunderhead Mountain, an elevation gain of more than twelve hundred feet from Spence Field. Day three called for the pair to follow the Appalachian Trail east to Silers Bald and, not far east of that, to turn right into North Carolina on the Welch Ridge Trail. This would be a mostly downhill walk, ending on the Lakeshore Trail at Fontana Lake, and it would be a long slog, calling for them to cover about twelve miles. The following day they planned to go west on Lakeshore Trail to the Jenkins Ridge Trail, which would take them uphill back to Spence Field, after which they would return to their car the following day. Unfortunately, they did not follow their plan.

The friends hiked up to Spence Field on May 6 and spent the night as planned. The next day, the 7th, they set off for Derrick Knob. The Appalachian Trail follows the high crest of the Great Smoky Mountains but that does not mean it is level; the trail rolls up and down to ascend and then descend peaks. As the two hiked along they decided the route they had planned involved too much gaining, losing, and regaining altitude, so they got out their map and a compass and planned an off-trail shortcut. At first the woods were open but, as is common in the Smoky Mountains, this did not last long. Soon the two were thrashing through the heavy vegetation in the drainage of the west fork of Roaring Fork Branch. As they went along other streams joined Roaring Fork and they had to find a way across these tributaries.

Walt was a faster walker than Rick and the two gradually became separated, although they kept in touch with shouts and occasional glimpses of each other. Eventually they found an old logging railroad bed parallel to the creek. The walking became more level, but the brush was just as thick as ever and the contacts between the two grew farther and farther apart. When Rick found himself alone, he made one of the classic maneuvers of people who are lost: He began to go in circles. When rain began to fall he made a good decision, stopping and making as good a camp as he could. Unfortunately, his poncho had been tied to the outside of his pack, and his rain gear had been shredded by the brush he had forced his way through. Rick was now off the route the two had followed earlier in the day.

Walt eventually became concerned about his hiking companion and stopped to wait for him. When Rick did not appear in a reasonable time, Walt went back to search for him and, in order to speed up his pace, put his pack down. As darkness came on he could not find Rick, nor could he find his pack. Thoroughly wet with sweat and from crossing numerous streams, Walt soon faced a further soaking from the rain.

The following day, still separated from each other, Rick tried to retrace his steps but found the challenge of bush-whacking uphill too much. In his exhausted state, he began to abandon what equipment he had remaining, including food. Walt had the good luck to find his pack, but he spent much of the day wandering around looking for Rick. Late in the afternoon he discovered the Hall Cabin, an intact structure on the Hazel Creek Trail, which provided him shelter for the night.

On May 9 Walt made a good decision. Time was passing, Rick was likely in trouble, and help was needed. Using his map he saw that he could junction with the Lakeshore Trail and then follow the route the two had originally planned to get back to Cades Cove. It would be a long, hard day, but his motivation to help his friend drove him on. At about 8:00 p.m., after hiking up one side of the main ridge of the Smoky Mountains and then down the other, Walt reached the Cades Cove Ranger Station and initiated a search. Rick had spent the day making very little distance because he was very tired and because he was still bushwhacking. Being on a trail makes an enormous difference in how fast a hiker can walk and how much ground can be covered.

On May 10 searchers, assisted by helicopters, dog teams, and the expert man tracker Dwight McCarter, went to the point where Walt and Rick had left the Appalachian Trail to take their "shortcut" across country. Soon the searchers were following occasional footprints and the dogs were following a strong scent trail. As they reached the banks of Roaring Fork and moved downstream, they began to find items Rick had lost as well as scraps of his rain gear he had used in a Hansel and Gretel attempt to mark his trail. Because Rick had wandered around a lot, the trail was confusing and the searchers wound up at the Hall Cabin where Walt had spent the night earlier. The following day the search party reversed its course and followed the clues Rick had left, some deliberately and some of them inadvertently. By night the trail had been lost on rocky ground and a halt was called.

Early the next morning a helicopter crew spotted Rick on top of a ridge and, although the terrain did not allow it to land, it hovered over the spot until searchers on foot could arrive. Rick was in acceptable physical condition, but he was mentally upset and it took some time for him to help his rescuers understand what had happened to him. Rick was able to walk to the Appalachian Trail and to follow it to a place where an air evacuation could be made.

Walt and Rick went in together. If they had stayed together, their experience would have been much less harrowing; if they had stayed on the trail there would have been no unpleasant experiences at all, only sore muscles. When the prospect of hiking uphill became unappealing, a good decision would have been to return to their car, following established trails.

—◆—

Here is what happens when a group stays together. October is a grand time to be in the Great Smoky Mountains. The air is like crisp wine, the sun is warm but not at all hot, and the leaves are a glorious riot of color. On October 18, 2014, George and Heather Ferrell and their four children, ages four, five, ten, and twelve, set off for a fun day in the woods. They planned to climb Mount LeConte, one of the highest peaks in the park, on top of which is situated Mount LeConte Lodge, a rustic accommodation that provides meals and a place to sleep. The lodge is so popular with hikers that reservations must be made as much as a year in advance. The Ferrell family did not plan to spend the night at the lodge; they were out for a day hike during which they would ascend Mount LeConte by way of the Rainbow Falls Trail and return via the Bullhead Trail.

Rainbow Falls Trail begins on the Cherokee Orchard Road in the park near Gatlinburg, passes Rainbow Falls, and continues to a junction with Bullhead Trail not far from the summit of Mount LeConte and LeConte Lodge. The trail is steep in places and can be muddy as it gains 3,820 feet from the trailhead to the top of the mountain, having covered more than six and a half miles.

Bullhead Trail, as noted, follows the same track as Rainbow Falls for the last part of the hike up the mountain but splits off as one comes down the mountain, leading to the same trailhead as Rainbow Falls but taking just over seven miles to get to that point. The Ferrell family had planned a day hike of more than thirteen and a half miles with two young children and two others who had limited strength; they had bitten off more than they could chew.

The family made it to the top of Mount LeConte, although the children needed help from time to time. They made it back down to the trail junction and took the proper path, following the Bullhead Trail, and then things began to go wrong. Energy was about gone for all the party, especially the younger children, their food had all been eaten, and clouds were rolling in. They still had a long way to go to reach their vehicle.

When it gets dark in the Smoky Mountains, it gets dark in a hurry. The official hour of sundown is not important; a hiker needs to have a good idea of when it gets "woods dark." The sun can dip below a ridge, the trees begin to throw heavy shadows, and it is dark in the woods some time before official sundown. The Ferrells found themselves walking and walking through a shadowy, increasingly dark forest and the trail's end was nowhere in sight. They went on as long as they could, but darkness, lack of food, and exhaustion finally forced them to stop. But they stayed together and they stayed on the trail.

The Bullhead Trail has an interesting feature; as a hiker gets farther up the side of Mount LeConte, the town of Gatlinburg comes into view. The town had not been visible during the day because of the leaves on the trees, but at night the glow of its lights could be seen. Where there are lights there is probably a cellphone tower. A light rain had begun to fall and the temperature was dropping, heading for a low of 28 degrees—when you stand on the park boundary in Gatlinburg you are in Tennessee, but when you get on top of LeConte you are in Canada as far as the climate is concerned. George was desperate to do something to help his family, so he pulled out his cellphone, and joy of joys, he got a signal. When he dialed 911 the Emergency Service in Pigeon Forge answered. George did not know his precise location and the signal faded in and out, but he managed to make heard the words Rainbow Falls and Bullhead Trail.

Park headquarters received a call from the Pigeon Forge Emergency Service a little after 2:00 a.m., and rangers were sent to make a "hasty search" of both trails. A "hasty search" is just what it sounds like; rangers quickly follow the designated trails to see if the lost party can be found on the trail. Of course it took some time to rouse park personnel from sleep, get them to the trailhead, and for them to climb up the path toward the top of the mountain. A few minutes after 7:00 a.m. rangers found the cold, wet, hungry, but safe family. They were taken back to LeConte Lodge, about a mile away, given breakfast and dry clothes, and, after a rest, they walked back to their car.

No doubt this will be a family legend repeated for many years. It has a happy ending because the Ferrell family went in together and they came out together. They were able to do that because they stayed on the trail and because they got lucky—they were able to pick up a cellphone signal.

A shorter hike would have been more appropriate as would have been the precaution of carrying extra food, water, and rain gear, but following a simple rule made all well in the end.

Like most searches for lost people in the Great Smoky Mountains, the search for the Ferrell family did not take long. The Park Service has an excellent record of finding people, especially if they stick to the trails. Some searches are over even quicker than the search for the Ferrells.

⌒⌒

Christy Barns and her teenage son, Casey, drove to Clingmans Dome on June 7, 2015. They were out for a day hike at one of the most popular locations in the Great Smoky Mountains National Park. Hundreds of people visit Clingmans Dome every day during the summer; there is a large parking area, restrooms, a gift shop, and an observation tower offering panoramic views of the park. The Appalachian Trail passes near the observation tower and, from the parking area, the Forney Ridge Trail leads to Andrews Bald, an area likely to be covered with blooming mountain laurel, rhododendron, and flame azaleas in early June.

The two Wisconsin residents seem to have sampled the more popular attractions, including the observation tower, and then they set off into the woods, even though they did not seem to have a fixed destination. They enjoyed the day, but the sun was declining toward the west and they did not know where they were, so they could not know the way back. Then they did something very contemporary; they sent a text message to a member of their family saying they were lost and needed help.

The family received the text message just after 8:30 p.m., and park headquarters was immediately called. Thirty rangers converged on Clingmans Dome, located the Barns's car, and began a hasty search of all the trails running through the vicinity. Less than five hours later the missing pair was found sitting beside the Forney Ridge Trail.

Go in together, stick together, stay on the trail, and come out together. Even better, have a good idea of where you are going, get a map from a visitor center, and put a flashlight in your pocket just in case.

Two families were very lucky because they managed to use their cellphones. This was luck since cellphone signals are spotty and generally weak in the mountains. Hikers should never depend on cellphones to get them out of a jam.

CHAPTER 9

Vanished Without a Trace

IT SOUNDS IMPOSSIBLE BUT IT DOES HAPPEN. SOMETIMES people simply vanish as if they were gone from the face of the earth. There are numerous cases in which it has later been determined that the disappearances were carefully planned and carried out for a variety of reasons. But, sometimes people seem to disappear for no reason at all. Since national parks across the nation draw a very large number of visitors annually, it is not surprising that a number of these cases involve the parks and, since the Great Smoky Mountains are the most frequently visited of all national parks, it is to be expected that the Smoky Mountains have their share of such cases. In all such cases search efforts are made, but if no clues are found the case eventually has to be closed and the search called off. This means that sometimes people have to be assumed to be dead. These cases are always tragic for the families of the vanished person, but when the person is a teenager, the matter becomes especially poignant. Trenny Lynn Gibson is one such case.

The biology class for juniors at Bearden High School in Knoxville, Tennessee, was going on a field trip on October

8, 1976. Wayne Dunlap was the teacher of the class, and he had made the trip more appealing to his students by saying that the destination would remain a mystery until the students were ready to depart. The purpose of the trip was to observe the diversity of plant life to be found at the chosen location. The Knoxville area is an ideal location for observing a variety of plant life, since a drive of from a few minutes to a couple of hours provides access to riverine environments, upland forests, rolling farmlands, or to the heights of the Great Smoky Mountains.

The weather forecast for the day was unusual for early October; cool temperatures with a chance of rain and fog were predicted. Although the students did not know where they were bound, the forecast was good reason to take warm clothes. Students brought their lunch with them, but there was no need for money so many of the young people were not carrying purses or wallets, just a little spending money in their pockets.

By 8:00 a.m. the class members were all present and a bus was waiting for them. Dunlap got everyone on board and then told them they were headed for the high country of the Great Smoky Mountains National Park. Their destination was the parking area at Clingmans Dome, from which they would take the trail to Andrews Bald, one of the naturally occurring areas in the Smoky Mountains that are devoid of tree cover and are home to a variety of grasses, shrubs, and flowers. The students were told they did not have to stay in a single group, but they were to go no farther than Andrews Bald and they were to be back at the bus by 3:30 p.m. for the return trip to Knoxville. Mr. Dunlap was the only adult chaperone on the trip, although a bus driver was assigned to handle the vehicle. The driver would be responsible for the safe operation of the vehicle but had no responsibility to assist with the students.

It took a little time for the school bus to clear the morning traffic and to drive to the park; there was a rest stop and that took some time, so the class did not arrive at Clingmans Dome until 12:30. This left three hours to make a 3.8-mile round-trip hike to Andrews Bald. The students were reminded of the time limits and then they were off.

Some of the students went at a faster pace than others, some hustled down the trail just happy to have a day out of school, while others took more seriously the assignment to observe the plant life. Soon the class was broken up into small groups, each going at its own rate of speed. On the trip from the school to the park Trenny had shared a seat with another student, Robert Simpson. They were friends and had gone on short rides in Knoxville in Robert's car. When the hike began Trenny and Robert were in the same small group and walked together out to the bald, eating their lunch along the way. They did not return together as Robert wanted to stay a little longer at their destination, despite the onset of a light rain, and the rest of his group left him to return with other students.

Andrews Bald is located on the Forney Ridge Trail, which begins at the Clingmans Dome parking area and runs for over five miles into the park, ending at a junction with the Springhouse Branch Trail. Just over a mile from the parking area where the trail begins, there is a junction with the Forney Creek Trail that continues over ten miles to the shores of

Fontana Lake on the southern edge of the park. Just a short distance from the trailhead another trail goes north and west for about a mile to junction with the Appalachian Trail. All trail junctions are clearly signposted today and were in 1976. Andrews Bald is an unmistakable destination, since the trail has traversed heavy woods from the trailhead until it suddenly emerges into the open area of the bald. There is little or no chance that a person could have taken a wrong turn and wandered deeper into the park so long as they remained on the marked trails.

At some point during the day Trenny had borrowed a heavy jacket from a classmate, a brown plaid garment which did not match her blue blouse and sweater but which was warm. Several of her fellow students remembered her wearing the jacket when she, along with other small groups, left Andrews Bald at about 2:00 p.m. As the students wended their way back toward their bus Trenny was going faster than some of the others, so she walked for short distances with several groups. At one point Trenny was accompanied by Bobbie Coghill and the two overtook two other classmates. Someone suggested a short rest, but Trenny kept going by herself. This occurred about a half mile from the parking area at Clingmans Dome. As the group watched, Trenny got a little distance ahead and then, as one witness remembered, Trenny turned right off the trail. This happened about 3:00 p.m.

No trail leads to the right at the point where Trenny was seen turning. Of course, stepping off the trail for a short distance is the common practice when one needs to answer a call of nature.

Her classmates thought nothing of what they had seen until they arrived at the bus and found Trenny was not there. Nothing can be more disturbing to a teacher than to find a student missing from a field trip group, but Mr. Dunlap kept his head. When everyone else was present, about ten minutes past the assigned return time, the teacher organized a search by the students of the parking area, which is quite large, but gave strict instructions not to go beyond the bounds of that area. One student was sent back to Andrews Bald to double-check the trail and another volunteered to go west on the Appalachian Trail for two miles to the Double Springs Gap Shelter just in case Trenny had taken the side trail that connects the route to Andrews Bald with the Appalachian Trail. Wayne Dunlap got on his Citizens Band Radio (this was before the day of cellphones) and contacted the Park Service, which sent a ranger to take control of the search. Mr. Dunlap made his first report at 4:06, and the ranger arrived at 4:30 p.m. With Dunlap staying behind to help in the search, the bus returned to Knoxville, leaving Clingmans Dome at about 5:00 p.m.

For some reason, no one notified the Bearden High School principal until the bus arrived back at the school, two and a half hours after leaving Clingmans Dome, a little after 8:00 p.m. A guidance counselor from the school telephoned the Gibson home with the news their daughter was missing. Mrs. Hope Gibson was home alone when the call came; her husband, Robert, was on a business trip and was not expected to arrive until 9:00 when his plane would land at McGhee Tyson Airfield in Knoxville.

By full darkness a search had been organized. The weather had deteriorated, with heavy rain and falling temperatures.

On his arrival Mr. Gibson and his wife contacted park head-quarters and were told to come to the park, bringing with them clothes worn by Trenny so search dog teams could have a scent to follow.

By the following morning a full-scale search was under-way with volunteers, park personnel, the Red Cross, and dog search teams all on hand. By afternoon the weather had moderated enough that an air search could be undertaken using Tennessee National Guard helicopters. A careful search of the Point Last Seen revealed no scent the dogs could follow, only an empty beer can and three cigarette butts, the sort of trash unfortunately found all too often along park trails.

On the second day a surprising report was made to Robert and Hope Gibson. One of the dog teams had followed their daughter's scent along the road leading from Clingmans Dome toward Newfound Gap for over a mile and a half. This scent trail was followed on successive days by other dog teams as a double-check on the first finding. Cigarette butts of the same brand as those found on the trail were discovered at the roadside location where the scent trail gave out. Since there was at least the possibility of a kidnapping or foul play, the Park Service informed the Federal Bureau of Investigation because federal authorities have jurisdiction over park property.

Over the next few days the Gibsons shared a story with the FBI that raised the level of suspicion of kidnapping or worse. Some two years earlier a young man had wanted to date Trenny and had actually broken into her bedroom late one night. Hope Gibson had heard the intruder, got a gun, and went to investigate. In a confrontation she shot the young man in the foot and, when the police arrived, he was arrested. He was convicted and sentenced to spend time in jail, but made public threats at his trial to harm Trenny on his release. School records, however, showed that the young man had been in class in Knoxville all day on the day of the field trip.

As would be expected, there were several reports of possible sightings of people who looked like Trenny, but investigations of each of these leads found that the person seen was really someone else. With no viable leads the search ended in late October.

Mr. Robert Gibson was a man with political connections, and he used those connections to bring about a second search for his missing daughter in April and May of the following year. This effort was as unsuccessful as the first, since the intervening winter weather destroyed any remaining clues.

Did Trenny Gibson walk along the Clingmans Dome road, unseen by her classmates, and get in a car with a person she knew? Did she leave the trail to answer a call of nature and become confused, wandering farther and farther into the wilderness? Was she abducted, as her father feared? Her case is one of presumed dead, but certainly vanished.

If a person wanted to deliberately disappear, the Great Smoky Mountains National Park would be an ideal location for such a vanishing act. There are over eight hundred square miles of rugged terrain, most of which is covered with dense vegetation. But there is no evidence that Trenny Gibson wanted to disappear; neither is there any such evidence in a later case involving fifty-eight-year-old Thelma Pauline Melton.

Polly Melton, as she was always known, and her husband, Robert, lived in their Airstream mobile home. The sleek, shiny aluminum trailer was not large, but it was well designed and provided a good home for them. The Meltons had been married for six years, both having been previously wed. Polly had no children by her first marriage, but Robert had two sons and Polly retained close ties with her father. Polly and Robert made their home base Jacksonville, Florida, where they spent part of the year and where they rented a storage unit for seasonal items they wanted on occasion but which they did not wish to carry with them at all times.

People who live a nomadic life using travel trailers often form close communities with which they associate from place to place as they travel across the country. The Meltons were part of such a group. The same families spent each summer at a private campground on the North Carolina side of the park, near the Deep Creek section of the Smoky Mountains. Since the group stayed for several months, they utilized a private campground because the Park Service places a time limit on the occupancy of its sites. This part of the park is quieter than the Trans-Mountain Road area that connects Gatlinburg, Tennessee, and Cherokee, North Carolina. Most of the ten million annual visitors to the park drive the Trans-Mountain Road, stopping at Newfound Gap and taking a side trip from the Gap out to Clingmans Dome. On another day most visitors will also drive the Little River Road toward the Townsend Wye and then follow the road to Cades Cove where a loop road gives impressive views of the cove and its surrounding mountains. But many fewer visit the Deep Creek area, most of them being serious hikers and fly fishermen, although on weekends the picnic area beside Deep Creek draws numerous day-trippers as local people visit the park.

On September 25, 1981, the close-knit cluster of travel trailer dwellers had already been in the area since May. They would be staying a little longer to enjoy the fall colors and crisp air and then the group would break up and go separate ways for the winter. About 3:00 p.m. on this day, Polly met two of her friends for a walk in the park; they were going to follow the Deep Creek Trail into the park for a ways and then turn back, making a loop of about four miles. The friends who were going with Polly were Trula Gudger and Pauline (Red) Cannon. Before leaving their campground Polly prepared sauce for the spaghetti she was planning for dinner for her and Robert. Then the trio set off.

Although the friends were planning a four-mile walk, it was not a strenuous route. The Deep Creek Trail is actually an old road in the section they were planning to cover, and it was a route they had walked many times. Also, they were not interested in strenuous hiking. Polly had some medical conditions, including high blood pressure and nausea, for which she took medicine. She was also a heavy smoker, going through some two packs of cigarettes every day. The three were all dressed in casual clothes, but Polly had on a pair of shoes of which the left shoe had a crack across the ball of her foot. This meant she would leave very distinctive footprints.

When the group reached the place where they had decided to turn around and head back to their campers, they paused for a short rest and then took the road back, chatting and gossiping about various inconsequential matters. After several hundred yards of strolling along, Polly suddenly accelerated her pace and began to leave her companions behind, but Trula and Red thought this was a joke, that Polly would soon be out of breath and would slow down, allowing them to overtake her. The trail passes over several slight rises and Polly disappeared over one of these. Her friends knew there was a bench alongside the trail just over the hill, and they fully expected to find her there. But when they arrived, there was no Polly.

There was still no cause for worry, Polly was just walking faster than usual, they thought. But when they reached their campground and stopped at the Meltons trailer, Robert told them he had not seen Polly since the three of them left on their walk. A quick look revealed that Polly was not in the campground, so her friends and Robert organized an informal search party of a few people and walked back along the Deep Creek Trail. From the point where Polly was last seen to the end of the Deep Creek Trail, there are no intersecting trails that Polly could have taken by mistake, even if she had become disoriented by her medical conditions; there are numerous short paths leading a few feet to the banks of the creek and these were all looked into. By 6:00 p.m., less than two hours after last being seen, a report was filed with the ranger on duty at Deep Creek that Polly was missing.

As darkness fell over the Deep Creek area, the Park Service began to organize a search. Because most of the route followed by the three friends had been over an old road, and because some of that road was outside the park and was open to vehicle traffic, the chance of finding signs of Polly's passage were very small unless she had gone off trail. By daylight on the next day, dog teams and volunteers, as well as park personnel, assembled to continue the search. The weather was dry, as is usually the case in September, and the dog teams had great difficulty getting any scent of Polly. In addition, no obvious places were found where a person had broken bushes or other vegetation in going off trail. In short, there was simply no clue as to where Polly Melton might have gone. The search continued for most of the week with the Deep Creek Trail being closed to the public in an attempt to preserve any clues. None were found.

Because there are several deep pools of water along Deep Creek, people who swam and fished in the stream were asked to keep a lookout for any sign of Polly as a drowning victim. No reports were ever received.

Speculation among Polly's friends and in public media raised the possibility of her being abducted or having met someone with whom she willingly ran away. The conclusion of such discussion was that Polly was happy in her relationship with her husband and was not at all likely to have run away from him. The FBI decided there was no evidence of a kidnapping and that they had no basis on which to conduct an investigation. To this day, Polly Melton is simply someone who walked over the crest of a slight hill and disappeared. The Great Smoky Mountains keep her secret yet.

Every year about five hundred thousand people are reported missing in the United States, and at any given time law enforcement officials are working about eighty thousand active cases. About four in ten of these are children who run away or who are taken by a parent who does not have legal custody of the child.

Most of the adults who go missing have substance abuse problems or are suffering from dementia or Alzheimer's. The remainder of the missing persons tend to be people escaping some kind of legal bind or running from the law. A very few cases, about six annually for the Great Smoky Mountains National Park, are people who have decided to take their own lives. These suicides usually occur in areas near or along park roads and usually the deceased leaves a vehicle to mark the spot where they entered the forest. Neither Trenny Gibson nor Polly Melton seems to fit any of these categories.

Such cases fuel the imagination of conspiracy theorists, UFO advocates, and those who track "Bigfoot," and entire books, as well as numerous websites, can be found propounding these theories. There have even been proposals that "wild men" still inhabit the recesses of wilderness areas such as those found in national parks and are responsible for unsolved disappearances.

Most of those who disappear in national parks are soon found, and of those who are not, or who are found deceased, most have been the victims of disorientation, dehydration, or hypothermia, all of which are very real dangers to anyone who goes into the woods alone or who goes off trail. But those who are presumed dead because they simply vanished remain intriguing mysteries.

CHAPTER 10

Murder in the Mountains

THE GREAT SMOKY MOUNTAINS NATIONAL PARK IS A SAFE
place. Even with ten million visitors annually, there are few
deaths. When lives are lost it is usually the result of an accident such as a vehicle crash or drowning. Very seldom is
there a crime involving serious bodily injury, much less loss
of life, and most visitors are as safe in the Smoky Mountains
as they are in their home neighborhoods. The incidents discussed in this chapter are quite unusual; after all, the park is
more than eighty years old, and there have been only three
cases of homicide and one case in which a wanted man made
use of the mountains to escape from the law.

On March 2, 1976, a fire watcher in a lookout tower
saw smoke rising from an area only about a mile away along
North Carolina State Route 94. A North Carolina Forestry
Service ranger named Ronald Brickhouse responded to the
report and found two or three acres of brush and young pine
trees ablaze. After taking a quick look at the situation, the
ranger decided that the fire was too large for one person to
handle, so he returned to his truck to radio for help. As he
made his way back, he noticed something he had missed on

his first quick inspection; there was a hole in the earth and in it were two bodies, badly charred but still smoldering. A gas can stood nearby along with a shovel, and the ground held fresh tire tracks. The weather had been wet for some time before this incident so the woods had not immediately caught on fire, and it was possible that the bodies had been set on fire as much as an hour before being found.

Ranger Brickhouse made his first call to the sheriff instead of to his fellow rangers, and the county sheriff, with two assistants, came to the scene. Once he had seen the pit containing the bodies, the sheriff immediately called on the State Bureau of Investigation for help and that agency sent officers to the scene. Much to the horror of all present, when the two visible bodies were lifted from the pit, three bodies of children were seen under them. Despite attempts to control the flow of information, rumors were soon rife over all the small surrounding communities.

A full-blown investigation began the following day with more than a dozen State Bureau of Investigation agents making door-to-door inquiries to determine if there were any missing locals who might be the victims. Meanwhile, the bodies had been removed for autopsies to a large hospital in Chapel Hill, North Carolina. The medical examiner determined that four of the victims, three boys and a young woman, had met their deaths as a result of being beaten with a heavy, blunt instrument. The fifth body was that of an older woman who had only slight wounds, and it was surmised she had died of a heart attack induced by fright.

Bulletins sent to law enforcement officials in the surrounding region did not get any responses concerning five missing persons, so the search was slowly widened. They began to search through dental records, but this was a slow, tedious process since there was no limited focus for the search and the entire region had to be covered. Then a break came from an unexpected place. The shovel found at the site of the fire still had part of the manufacturer's tag glued to the handle. A hardware store owner told the police which company manufactured the shovel, and through the manufacturer the police traced the shovel to a store in Bethesda, Maryland. The store employees did not recognize the pictures of any of the victims, they could not remember who had bought the shovel, and the purchase had been made in cash, leaving no paper trail. But the North Carolina authorities did begin asking questions in the Bethesda area. Soon they had an ID. A neighbor had reported not having seen any of the family who lived next door for about a week. The officer sent to knock on the door found blood on the porch steps, so a warrant was issued to allow police to enter the house. There was blood in almost every room, and the police learned the husband of the family had not shown up for work in over a week.

The house belonged to Bradford Bishop, who lived there with his wife, Annette, his three sons, William, Brenton, and Geoffrey, and Lobelia Bishop, the mother of Bradford and the paternal grandmother of the three boys. Bradford Bishop was employed by the State Department in Washington, DC. According to the neighbors the Bishops had been a happy family who were engaged in sports and community activities. Bradford was a graduate of Yale, while his wife, Annette, had graduated from the University of California–Berkeley.

Bradford held a high-paying job and the family lived in a house valued at $100,000 (in 1976 dollars). Lobelia Bishop had become a widow only a few months earlier and had moved in with her son, but she had made herself quite useful, doing the cooking and taking the children to school and to after-school events, which allowed her daughter-in-law to pursue art classes at the nearby branch of the University of Maryland. The only disappointment anyone uncovered was that Bishop had learned on March 1 that he would not get a promotion he very much wanted, and that the rest of his career at the State Department would probably be spent in a desk job. Perhaps there were other stresses beneath the surface of normalcy, because it was later found Bishop had been under the care of a psychiatrist.

With a connection now established leading from Maryland to North Carolina, law enforcement agencies began to follow the paper trail Bishop had left. Credit card slips for gas, camping gear, and shoes were recovered and showed that Bradford Bishop had traveled in the area where the bodies had been found. Then came an important discovery. On March 18 a ranger in the Elkmont Campground noticed a vehicle that appeared to have been sitting in the same place for several days. No one paid any attention to the vehicle at first, because at that time there were still privately occupied summer homes at Elkmont that the owners had been allowed to keep under a lease agreement when the park was formed. But this vehicle was found not to belong to the residents of the summer houses and seemed to have not been moved for a long time. A check of the license plates showed the vehicle belonged to Bradford Bishop.

While investigators looked over the automobile, finding bloodstains and a bloody tarp probably used to hide the bodies, other police and park rangers closed the campground and brought in dogs to see if they could track Bishop. There was no scent trail leading from Bishop's car and nothing was found in the immediate area. Two popular trails, the Little River Trail and the Jakes Creek Trail, begin at the edge of Elkmont Campground and they intersect with other trails leading into the heart of the park. The dogs found nothing along the two trails leading from the campground, so the campground was reopened. Since the car had been abandoned for some days it was not likely that Bishop was in the immediate area, but searches in the backcountry continued for some time. Authorities knew that Bishop had been an avid outdoorsman and that he had done extensive camping in Africa, so it was assumed he had the skills to navigate and survive in the park. But time passed and Bradford Bishop was not found—and he never would be.

Did Bishop drop off his car in the Smoky Mountains and then walk some distance to another site to steal a car or, possibly, meet someone who gave him a ride? Did he go into the woods to hide and lose his own life to the forces of nature? Is it possible that Bishop took on a new identity and lived for many years under a false name? Numerous reports of sightings of Bishop have been reported over the intervening years, but no positive identification has ever been made. As late as 2014 a "John Doe" was exhumed in Scottsboro, Alabama, because it was decided his picture bore a strong physical resemblance to Bishop; DNA from a cigarette butt taken from Bishop's car was compared to DNA from "John

Doe," but there was no match between the two samples. The case is cold but not closed.

The Smoky Mountains were not the scene of Bradford Bishop's horrible crime, that occurred over three hundred miles away, but the vastness of their wilderness has helped to make the fate of Bradford Bishop a mystery. Some people with long memories still speculate that the bones of Bishop lie somewhere in the park. While the Bishop case remains officially open, although very cold, two cases involving homicide in the park were solved quickly.

Albert Brian Hunt lived near Arcadia, Florida, and loved the outdoors. Since spring was well underway by late April 1981, he decided he would visit the Smoky Mountains to get a change of scenery from the flat landscape of Florida and to do a little fishing. Albert enjoyed the trip, driving leisurely, stopping in Nantahala National Forest before arriving in the Smoky Mountains. He had decided to stay on the Cherokee side of the mountains in North Carolina. Along the way Albert had met two men whom he accepted as traveling companions, Robert Elton Taylor and Freddie Ray Staton.

Taylor and Staton were from the western part of North Carolina but they were rootless, having no regular jobs but having a number of bad habits including drug use. The pair noticed that Albert was driving a new car and, when they went to a store, they noticed that he had a good deal of money in his wallet. The idea of easy money apparently convinced the two to kill Albert, rob him, and take his car. On the night of May 2, they seem to have made a plan as to how they could do this and still conceal the body.

Early on May 3 Taylor and Staton told Albert they knew of a very special place to fish, one that was so far off the beaten path that no other anglers were likely to be found there, and they offered to be his guides to the location. They left their campsite in Smokemont Campground and drove through the park, passing Newfound Gap, stopping a short distance into Tennessee where Walker Camp Prong crosses the road. Taking their fishing rods, the trio parked the car at a pull-off and started following Walker Camp Prong upstream. There is no trail along the creek and the going soon became slow and difficult because of the thick vegetation. The tales of huge trout just waiting to take the hook kept Albert following his companions farther and farther into the woods.

The ultimate fishing hole was described to Albert as being "just above a little waterfall" and soon such a feature came into sight. As Albert made ready to cast a fly into the stream, Staton and Taylor attacked him. Staton got behind Albert and hit him on the back of the head with a large rock, either killing him or mortally wounding him. Rifling the pockets of the unconscious or dead man, they took the car keys and cash and made their way back to the road.

Back in Florida, Mrs. Hunt was concerned since she had not heard from Albert in several days. He had not telephoned as he had promised, so she called the police. A search alert was put out for Albert. That very same day Staton and Taylor had driven Albert's new car to Lawrenceville, Georgia, just a few miles east of Atlanta, and had tried to sell it. When they could not find a buyer because they did not have the proper documents showing they owned the vehicle, they drove it to a remote location and set fire to it. The fire caught the attention of residents in the area who called the police and they, in turn, traced the vehicle to Albert Hunt.

Taylor had been quite open in his efforts to sell the car, so it was not difficult for the police to track him down. He was arrested on June 4, one month after the murder. In his statement to the police, Taylor implicated Staton, who had left the area but was later found and arrested in Illinois in August 1981. Taylor then made a very strange bargain; he was told that if he helped the police find the remains of Albert Hunt and clear up the case, he would not be charged with auto theft. Taylor agreed!

On July 10, 1981, Taylor led agents from the FBI (the crime was committed on federal property), police, and park personnel up Walker Camp Prong to the scene of the crime. On arriving, no body was to be found, but the park's expert tracker, Dwight McCarter, soon discovered bones and fragments of clothing, all that animal scavengers had left of the body. DNA showed the bones were those of Albert Hunt, and the blood on the clothes was his as well. With both men in custody grand jury proceedings began in Knoxville, and charges of murder were brought against both men. Taylor was astonished; he thought he had cleared himself when the police promised to drop the auto theft charges. By the spring of 1982, both Taylor and Staton had entered a plea of guilty to second-degree murder and had been sentenced to thirty-five years in prison.

In 1990 Staton appealed his conviction, but his appeal was denied. Both men remain in jail.

———

Joe Kolodski was a ranger in the Great Smoky Mountains National Park, but his duties sometimes involved working on the Blue Ridge Parkway, which has its southern entrance near Cherokee, North Carolina, at the edge of the Great Smoky Mountains National Park. On June 21, 1998, Ranger Kolodski responded to a call that a man with a gun was threatening visitors to the Big Witch overlook on the Parkway, some six miles outside the park. On arriving at the overlook, Kolodski found Jeremiah Locust, wearing jeans, no shirt, and carrying a rifle. Locust moved into the woods when the ranger arrived and Kolodski momentarily lost sight of him; then Locust reappeared and fired at the ranger. Locust was armed with a large-caliber hunting rifle and the slug tore through the protective vest Kolodski was wearing. Ranger Anthony Welch had just arrived and saw his fellow ranger fall, but Locust opened fire at him and he was forced to take cover behind his patrol car.

Locust suddenly stepped out of the woods and began to walk toward Welch, who fired his shotgun at Locust. Locust fired several shots back at Welch, blowing out the back window of his car, and Locust ran into the woods. More than seventy law enforcement officers hurried to the scene of the crime, and some four hours later a tribal game warden on the adjacent Cherokee reservation arrested the suspect, who was found to have been drinking. Locust was sentenced to life in prison. Ranger Kolodski had served with the Park Service for thirteen years and was thirty-six years of age. He was survived by his wife and three children.

To reach the Abrams Creek Campground, it is necessary to follow the Happy Valley Road. How ironic that such a pleasant name should be associated with murder, but on May 21, 2006, that was indeed the case. The Happy Valley Road leads off the Foothills Parkway on the northwestern shoulder of the Smokies and dead-ends not far into the park. The road is not a major route into the park and very few visitors drive it; Abrams Creek Campground is small, having only sixteen sites, so few of those touring the park even hear of the place. The campground attracts people who want to fish in Abrams Creek or who want a secluded location. On May 20 the sites in the campground were almost all full and quiet had fallen over the mountains, but the tranquility of the site was disturbed in the early morning hours by the sounds of cursing, yells, and scuffling. When some of the campers went to see what was causing the disturbance, they found a body.

By 4:15 a.m. deputies from the local sheriff's office had arrived, and the FBI had been called because federal property is within their jurisdiction. Since his wallet was still in his pocket, the dead man was quickly identified as Steven Lynn Davis from the nearby town of Greenback, Tennessee. Davis was not registered as a camper but had been visiting others, among them Joseph Moyers Jr., of Alcoa, Tennessee, also a nearby town. Investigators learned that Davis and Moyers had both been drinking and got into an argument. During the course of the confrontation, Moyers drew a knife and stabbed Davis. Moyers had been arrested eight months earlier in another stabbing incident.

Since the crime had been committed within a national park, Moyers was put on trial in the US District Court in Knoxville in 2006 and was ordered to be incarcerated in the Blount County, Tennessee, jail. In 2009 he appealed to the court, stating that his civil rights were being violated by being held in a county prison facility, but his appeal failed. Moyers served out his time.

Alcohol—allowed in the Great Smoky Mountains National Park for those of legal drinking age—seems to have been a factor in this particular incident. Obviously, overindulgence is never a good plan. The small size of the Abrams Creek Campground was also a factor in this case; its remote location means there is no ranger continuously on duty as is the case in the larger campgrounds in the park.

Just inside the Great Smoky Mountains National Park as a visitor drives from Cherokee, North Carolina, toward Tennessee, signs point to some historic buildings, many of them once part of the thriving community of Smokemont. One of those buildings is the Oconaluftee Baptist Church, founded in 1836 and which continued to exist as an active congregation until 1939 when the residents sold their land to the park. This church is also known as the Lufty (or "Luftee") Baptist Church.

To reach the church travelers turn off the Trans-Mountain Road at the entrance to Smokemont Campground and drive across the bridge over the Oconaluftee River. A pull-off to one side provides parking and there is a sign pointing to the church. Today the church building, erected about 1916, is an architectural monument and is used only for occasional weddings and family reunions. On March 29, 2015, the building became the scene of something much more sinister.

At 2:50 a.m. that day the 911 emergency service in Cherokee received a call from Tyler Britton Gaddis, a resident of Whittier, North Carolina. Tyler gasped that he was in the Lufty Baptist Church in the park and that he was badly hurt and needed help immediately. A call from the emergency service to the Smokemont Ranger Station got a ranger on the way immediately, but Tyler was dead when the ranger arrived.

The FBI undertook an investigation and found only numerous bloodstains from the deceased man. A medical examination of the body showed Tyler had been stabbed nineteen times with many of the wounds on his right hand and forearm, as if trying to deflect the weapon from a more vital spot.

A thorough search of the building found no other clues, and there were no footprints or tire tracks leading to the building, in short, there were no clues to go on. Interviews were conducted with the family and friends of the deceased, but they did not help the case forward; there were no witnesses who had seen Tyler in the area and, obviously, there were no leads as to whom he might have been with or whom he might have met. There was no reason for anyone to be in the church in the small hours of the morning, and speculation arose that some sort of covert business had brought two people there, though there are no facts to support this speculation. With no clues and no witnesses to assist them, the FBI continues to investigate the case.

Both recent cases involving homicides took place on the edge of the park and involved people who lived only a short distance away. This would suggest that there was some kind of argument or personal issue involved that made those involved a danger solely to themselves and not to most visitors to the park. While any national park has its share of petty crime, such as items being taken from unlocked cars, serious crimes are quite rare. Our national parks are at least as safe as our home neighborhoods.

———❦———

Bradford Bishop's car was found at Elkmont Campground, and as noted, speculation continues about his possible fate. Rumors and speculation about the park crop up on all manner of subjects. In 2015 a social media posting reporting the "discovery of a 100 year old lost town in the Smoky Mountains" went "viral." This "lost town" was actually the summer cabins adjacent to Elkmont Campground, which were once occupied by families who had convinced the Park Service to give them extended leases so they could keep their summer cabins. The Park Service stopped extending these leases some years ago, and most of the structures are slowly falling into ruins. Some of the buildings are being preserved by the Park Service for future public use. These buildings were hardly a "secret," since the Little River Trail and the Jakes Creek Trail lead dozens of hikers past them every week. The Smoky Mountains seem to lend themselves to mysteries, true or not.

CHAPTER 11

Don't Overestimate Your Ability

THE QUICKEST WAY TO GET IN TROUBLE IN THE OUTDOORS, especially in a rugged environment such as the Great Smoky Mountains National Park, is to overestimate your ability to face the challenges the mountains will present. Overestimate yourself, underestimate the mountains, and you are on a collision course with trouble. A brief article from a Knoxville, Tennessee, newspaper, dated November 13, 1995, tells the story starkly: "The body of an unidentified male, about 35, was found yesterday by two other hikers nears Pecks Corner on the Appalachian Trail in the Great Smokies. The cause of death has been ruled to be hypothermia." This was one of many similar incidents in the history of the park.

Cindy Hall and her husband were visiting the Smoky Mountains on a pre-Christmas excursion in 2009. They were not planning to do any serious hiking, but they were hoping to get some good pictures of ice and snow. The weather had accommodated them by providing low temperatures at night, so there were icicles dangling from rock faces and snow and ice atop rocks in some of the streams. The couple drove to the Greenbrier entrance to the park, traveled a short distance into the park, and left their car at a picnic area. They walked several hundred yards upstream along the banks of the Little Pigeon River, snapping photos of the stream and its winter ornaments. Cindy decided she could get a good picture from a rock that jutted a little way out into the stream, and since the rock seemed to offer good footing, she stepped out on it. The rock was actually covered with a thin sheet of ice and both her feet slipped, tumbling her into the frigid water. The rapid current swept her downstream with her husband in frantic pursuit, scrambling over the logs and rocks on the riverbanks. In less than five minutes, he caught up with Cindy and pulled her from the water. He tried valiantly to get her on her feet so they could walk to their car, which was barely out of sight, but hypothermia made Cindy unresponsive. She died less than fifteen minutes walk from their automobile.

On January 12, 2013, Richard Lemarr left Newfound Gap with plans to hike thirty miles to Davenport Gap, where he would meet a friend on January 14. When he did not arrive, a search was undertaken and his body was found on January 16 at Tricorner Knob Shelter on the Appalachian Trail. The medical examiner in the case stated that the cause of death was hypothermia. Since he was hiking alone, the details of his death can never be known, but inadequate preparation for the weather was clearly involved.

Weather in the Great Smoky Mountains can change quickly because the height of the mountains creates different climate zones as one ascends the slopes. In climbing some of the highest peaks, a hiker travels from the temperate zone of

Tennessee or North Carolina to a Canadian zone. Obviously, the temperature difference from the bottom of the mountain to its top can be great. Park officials point out that the weather forecast for the nearest town or city does not necessarily give a good picture of what will happen in the mountains. Nor does hypothermia strike only in the winter. A hiker drenched with sweat from a hard uphill trek on a summer's day can feel the effects of hypothermia if a chill breeze springs up, or if a sudden thunderstorm thoroughly wets his clothes and the temperature drops. During the busy spring and summer seasons, rangers are frequently called to help victims with mild cases of hypothermia, but those who need help in the winter require more effort on the part of the park since weather conditions can be much more challenging.

In 2014 rangers in the Great Smoky Mountains were involved in 104 search and rescue incidents involving 139 people. Most of these incidents involved hikers, but twenty-six incidents involved people who had gotten into difficulty because of insufficient information, errors in judgment, or insufficient clothing, equipment, or inadequate experience. Being prepared for unexpected challenges is necessary if an enjoyable hike is the goal. Even then, the challenge of the mountains may be more than a body can handle.

———

Jenny Bennett was a successful novelist and freelance editor who loved hiking in the Great Smoky Mountains. She belonged to a hiking club and had a large store of experience in traveling alone through the park, especially going off trail. Her love of hiking was also shared in a blog she maintained,

Endless Streams and Rivers. Jenny had lived in the Knoxville area for many years, beginning in the 1980s, then returned to her native Massachusetts because of family matters after just over ten years, then returned to Asheville, North Carolina, in the early 1990s. Not content to be simply near the mountains she loved, Jenny moved to Sylvia, North Carolina, shortly after 2000 where the park was practically her back door. Perhaps she was feeling a little sad, because she had just posted on her blog that she was moving to Vermont in a few weeks and would be leaving the Smoky Mountains behind.

The park had been the setting for her two novels, published in 2012 and 2014. The first was *Murder at the Jumpoff*, a mystery involving the death of an off-trail hiker whose body is found at the foot of a well-known landmark in the Smoky Mountains, a precipice called the Jumpoff. In the novel a park employee and a female detective from the local sheriff's department investigate the death and, in the process, the reader is led along many of the hiking trails in the vicinity of the Jumpoff.

Bennett's second novel was *The Twelve Streams of LeConte*. In this book a young woman loses her husband to another man while on her honeymoon. To find solace she decides to ascend Mount LeConte by following each of the twelve streams that flow down its sides. The book describes her relationships with three hiking companions as well as psychological insights the leading character has gained from her reading. Although fiction, *Twelve Streams* was based on the author's desire to perform such a feat.

Early in 2015 a fellow hiker and friend died and had requested that his ashes be scattered in a remote part of the park. Jenny was not able to participate in the ashes-scattering because she had knee problems. So, it may be, she went back to the mountains for a last visit before moving to Vermont and to pay her respects to her friend. Jenny entered the park at the Greenbrier entrance and parked her car at the Porters Flat Trailhead. Since she often hiked alone, no one knew she was missing until June 1 when her landlord called the local police. Jenny had agreed to vacate her rented house by June 1, and the landlord had sent some prospective renters to look at the house. They found it still filled with Jenny's possessions. The landlord was concerned that some accident had taken place, so a search was undertaken. The Park Service located Jenny's car on June 7, but the Porters Creek Trail serves a very large drainage and a person who liked to hike off trail could have gone anywhere. A search of trails and manways led to the discovery of Jenny's body on June 9 in the vicinity of Lester Prong, one of the streams that flow down from the Jumpoff area.

Jenny Bennett was not lost, she was not ill prepared; she was an experienced hiker who knew the challenges the mountains offer and she had often tested the limits of her ability. Did she simply give out; did this challenge overcome her?

———

Chestnut Top Trail is one of the best in the park for enjoying spring wildflowers, and April is usually the best month in which to enjoy them. Robert and Judith Lyons were visiting the park on April 11, 2009, and chose Chestnut Top for the beginning of their day hike, parking at the Wye where the road from Townsend and the Cades Cove Road split. They planned to follow the trail to School House Gap where they would junction with the School House Gap Trail, which would lead them out to the Cades Cove Road. Their planned route was about six and a half miles and involved about nine hundred feet in elevation gain, much of it gradual. However, about 250 feet of this elevation gain comes in the first few hundred feet of the trail as it climbs out of the Little River gorge, following a narrow footway with a steep drop on the right as one ascends.

On this particular day there were patches of snow in protected places and the trail was wet and muddy from snowmelt and some spring showers. A prudent hiker would have provided himself with a trekking pole, or even two, to help maintain balance and keep his footing under such conditions. Even the most agile hiker needs assistance under poor conditions. The couple had gone only a short way up the Chestnut Top Trail when a thunderstorm began to roll in from the west. Smoky Mountains thunderstorms can be quite violent because of the sudden updrafts created by the mountains. Lightning strikes along the ridges are frequent, and being caught in such a storm can be a challenging experience, so the couple made a wise decision; they turned back toward their car.

Somewhere along the steep section near the beginning of the trail, Robert lost his footing and fell down the steep slope for about twenty feet. Although his back hurt from an apparent injury, the couple made it back to their car and called the park dispatcher for help at about 5:30 p.m. Unfortunately, their location was given as the trailhead for School

House Gap, a location several miles from where they actually were. Perhaps confusing the names of the end of their route with their actual location at its beginning was caused by being overly excited, or perhaps it was caused by inadequate preparation in reading the trail guide and failure to look at a map. Rangers responding to the call went to School House Gap Trail and found no one. Meanwhile, Robert was in increasing pain and another call was made to park authorities at 6:10 p.m. This time the correct location was given and an ambulance arrived at 6:40. At Townsend, Robert was put aboard a helicopter and taken to a major hospital in Knoxville where he was pronounced dead at 10:20 p.m. He was seventy-three.

The Lyons had made a good decision in turning back when faced with poor trail conditions and deteriorating weather. The incorrect location given park rangers did delay the arrival of emergency aid, but it may have made no difference in this case. The same accident, with the same results, could have happened to a much younger person. Careful attention to equipment and to location are always needed. In the Great Smoky Mountains it is never wise to underestimate the challenges one may face.

Most search efforts in the Smoky Mountains result in the missing person being found in less than twenty-four hours. Sometimes they are found after a much longer time, but the rescue is still successful because the lost person has managed to survive a near-death event. On August 22, 2009, Albert Briggs, called "Morgan" by his friends, left his home

in Pigeon Forge near the park and registered at park headquarters for a weekend hike in the backcountry of the park.
Although Morgan was seventy years old, he was in good
physical condition and was an experienced hiker; he had
served as a "Ridge Runner," a volunteer who spent time on
the Appalachian Trail within the park boundaries providing
information to hikers, keeping an eye on what takes place
along the trail, and doing some trail maintenance. These volunteer crews spend five nights in the woods, then come out
for three nights, and return for a second shift of five nights.
At the time of his hike Morgan was working in the office
that issues permits for the use of backcountry campsites.
Since he was experienced, Morgan took to the woods properly equipped with good hiking boots, rain gear, food, water,
and a tent.

Morgan planned to enter the park in the Greenbrier section and spend his first night in the backcountry at Campsite
#31. The following day he wanted to take a manway called
the Dry Sluice, which leads up the main ridge of the mountains to the Appalachian Trail. Manways are not official
trails—they are not marked nor maintained—but off-trail
hikers often follow streambeds up the mountains creating a
route though not a distinct marked path. After reaching the
Appalachian Trail, Morgan planned to turn south to reach
the Icewater Springs Shelter, spend a night there, and then
take the Appalachian Trail and the Boulevard Trail to reach
Mount LeConte Shelter. That would be his last night on the
mountain, and he would come down the Alum Cave Bluff
Trail the following day to reach the Trans-Mountain Road
and, he trusted, catch a ride back to his home in Pigeon

Forge. He told neighbors to expect him home by Tuesday. When Morgan did not arrive, his neighbors alerted park officials and a search began.

As rangers began walking the trails looking for signs of Morgan, they met hikers who recalled seeing him at Campsite #31, but the rangers who visited Icewater Springs Shelter and Mount LeConte Shelter noted that he had not signed the register. This meant the search would concentrate on the off-trail section of his planned trip between the end of the Porters Creek Trail and the Dry Sluice manway. Careful ground searches found no clues as to what had happened to Morgan.

Although it was August, usually one of the driest months in the Smoky Mountains, air searches were hampered by fog and frequent rain showers. As events would prove, this was a very good thing. The search continued even though Morgan's planned route connected with a number of other trails he might have taken and all of them had to be walked to make sure he had not gone off his planned route. As the days went by, hope began to wane but persistence did not. On August 29, a week after Morgan had begun his hike, a search team on the Appalachian Trail was walking past Charlies Bunion, a well-known landmark on the trail, when one of the team noticed a yellow tent on a rock outcropping about a mile north of their location. There was no trail in that area, no backcountry campsite—so what was the tent doing there? A break in the weather allowed a helicopter to fly over the site and there was Morgan, waving a red handkerchief. The helicopter dropped food, water, and a two-way radio, and authorities began to plan how to get the lost hiker out of a very rugged place.

Good weather the next day allowed a visual inspection of the site from the air, and there was no place a helicopter could land. After a brief chat over the two-way radio, it was agreed that a rope with a seat would be lowered to Morgan and he would be hoisted 250 feet up to the helicopter. This was successfully accomplished and Morgan was soon reunited with his son. No medical attention was required and Morgan went home with his family.

Morgan had both used his abilities and had overestimated them. As he left the end of the Porters Creek Trail and took to the manway, he found himself traveling through a dense thicket of rhododendron and, in the process of crawling through it, he became disoriented. At this point, had he turned back and followed the streambed, he would have been back on the Porters Creek Trail in a relatively short time. Instead, he decided to keep climbing, perhaps thinking he had the ability to make it to the crest of the main ridge of the mountains and find the Appalachian Trail. Instead, Morgan summited Porters Mountain and found himself in such rugged terrain he could go neither up nor down. At this point the hiking ability Morgan had accumulated led him to do two things which were entirely correct: He stayed where he was and he began to ration his food. There was no water on top of the mountain, but the fog and rain allowed him to rig a tarp to catch water and funnel it into a pan from which he could fill his canteen.

Morgan Briggs used his abilities correctly in a number of ways that helped in his rescue. He told his neighbors where he was going and when they should expect him back. This allowed an alert to be sounded when he did not return on time. He filed a trip plan and got the required permits from park officials so they would have an idea of where they needed to look for him. He stayed calm, rationed his food, and collected water at every opportunity. Morgan overestimated his ability by tackling a manway alone and by continuing uphill when he lost his bearings. But, in the end, his skill and experience overcame the challenge of the mountains.

Brad Phillips had always wanted to hike part of the Appalachian Trail. In April 2015, he decided to do so with his son Clint and his son-in-law, Jason Wilbanks. The three men planned to hike up the main crest of the mountains to Spence Field and spend the night there. The weather looked favorable, so they left their car at a trailhead and went off into the woods. Brad was not in peak physical condition, and the mountains proved more of a challenge than he was ready to face. Walking up any of the Smoky Mountains is not like walking on a city sidewalk or even strolling on a greenway in a park. Trails usually have a rather rough surface with lots of roots and rocks, and a hike is likely to be a series of ups and downs as the rolling terrain of the mountainside is traversed with a steady overall gain in elevation. It takes a good deal of training and preparation to go on a hike and not feel physically challenged.

Then there is the weather. April is not to be depended on for good weather in the Smoky Mountains. A mild spring day can quickly turn wet and cold as a cold front pushing down from the north collides with warm, moist air pushing up from the Gulf of Mexico. April 5 was just such a day.

As the three men made their way up the mountain toward their destination of Spence Field, clouds began to roll in and their energy began to lag. Long before they reached their destination, Brad was exhausted; he could take only a few steps and then he would have to stop to rest. As the hikers watched, the clouds drew closer and lightning began to flash. They were about to experience one of the most awesome displays of nature in which one can ever be involved, a Smoky Mountains thunderstorm. The sudden rise of the mountains from the surrounding terrain causes tremendous updrafts, which can cause winds to blow uphill at high speeds. The sudden cooling of air as it rises over the mountains can cause deluges of water to fall, and each drop of water is fragmented by striking tree branches so that a person in the open becomes wet quickly and thoroughly. The thunder rolls and reverberates from mountain to mountain, making the storm sound even more fearsome than it may actually be.

Brad soon found himself at the end of his ability to continue. Taking shelter under a bush and covering himself as best he could, he told his companions to go on without him and try to find help.

Unknown to Brad, his son suffered a knee injury a few hundred yards ahead and his son-in-law had to continue alone. Alone, under his bush, with the storm raging, Brad thought his end had come so he began to pray. A hiker passing along the trail heard his prayer and managed to contact park officers. A "hasty search" along the trail led rangers to the injured man, and soon to his son as well.

During the night the weather broke and the next morning a Tennessee Highway Patrol helicopter lifted Brad out of the park to a local hospital, where he was soon joined by the rest of his family. He was released a short time later.

Overestimating one's physical ability and underestimating the challenge of the mountains almost brought about a tragedy. Good luck and good help prevented it from coming about.

———

David Roy and Mat Merten had climbed up the Alum Cave Trail on Mount LeConte, had reached their destination, and had turned back toward the trailhead. This was Roy's first hike on this particular trail. The Alum Cave Trail is one of the most popular trails in the park because it leads to several interesting features before reaching Alum Cave Bluff at two and a half miles from its beginning, then continuing another two and a half miles to reach the top of LeConte. Many families make the bluff their destination for a moderate day hike and then return to the parking area at the trailhead.

David and Mat reached the bluffs at about 7:00 p.m. and decided to stop for a quick bite to eat.

Although official sundown was still some time away, the light on the trail would soon fade because of the shadows cast by the mountains and the heavy forest cover through which the trail passes as it goes below the bluff. This meant they did not plan to stay long and, even so, would complete their hike in darkness. They had brought headlamps to illuminate their path and were prepared for night hiking on a developed trail.

While the two were eating their snack, they heard cries for help. The bluff is a concave formation, and from where they were sitting they could not pinpoint the origin of the cries. Unable to see the source of the pleas, they shouted to ask what was the matter. The response came from Angel Chaffin, an experienced hiker and an intern at the Great Smoky Mountains Institute, an educational facility within the park. Angel had hiked up to the bluffs and had decided to climb up them, and in the process she reached a place where she was afraid either to go ahead or to go back down. She was stuck.

Since David and Mat could not see Angel from their location at the foot of the bluffs, they followed the trail up the mountain for a short distance and tried to bushwhack back along the top of the precipice. By this time Angel had turned on her flashlight to help the two locate her, but the density of the vegetation and the ruggedness of the terrain separated the two would-be rescuers and they had to give up their attempt to reach the stranded climber. During their attempt to find their way back to the trail Mat fell, badly gashing his face. David did have the good luck to meet two hikers who agreed to make their best time to the trailhead and to go for help. David and Mat settled down to keep voice contact with Angel and to nurse as best they could Mat's injured face.

The two hikers who had gone for help were successful in their mission, reporting the incident at park headquarters at about 10:30 p.m. In the early hours of Sunday, park rangers arrived on the scene, allowing David and Mat to go for the medical help Mat needed (seven stitches were required to close the wound).

After a careful investigation of the location where Angel was stranded, the rangers decided to airlift her out and a helicopter was summoned. By early Sunday afternoon Angel was at the local airport where a quick medical examination showed she was in good physical condition, and she went back to work.

Angel was not a tyro at hiking or at climbing. She simply overestimated her ability, and it took four volunteers, a dozen park personnel, and a helicopter to get her back to safety.

Experienced hikers like Morgan Briggs and Angel Chaffin, as well as those who are not as well prepared, can easily make the mistake of overestimating their ability. Some escape the consequences of their act, but others pay the ultimate price. The challenges of the Great Smoky Mountains may be hidden beneath their beauty, but they are always there, ready to snare the unwary.

CHAPTER 12

Disaster Averted: The Blizzard of '93

MARCY PAISLEY HAD SPENT THE ENTIRE SEASON AT HER home in Detroit, and not once, all winter, had there been this much snow. The white stuff came up to her knees; the drifts were four feet deep in many places and as much as nine in others. Marcy was in a remote part of the Great Smoky Mountains National Park, but she was not alone. She was part of a group of 117 students and faculty from the private Cranbrook/Kingswood Upper Schools in Bloomfield Hills, a Detroit suburb. The group had traveled to the park as part of an annual event, which was based on concepts developed by the Outward Bound program.

Since 1971 Cranbrook had sponsored a ten-day camping and hiking event in the Great Smoky Mountains for some of its students. The group would arrive at the park by bus and break into small groups of fewer than a dozen students, with each group led by faculty members and senior students. The outing included such activities as hiking six miles a day, cooking meals on camp stoves, building campfires, and practicing outdoor skills. Such activities were designed to build self-confidence, self-esteem, and group cohesion. Participation in the event had become something of a rite of passage for the sophomore class members.

Cranbrook School leaders made careful preparations for the trip. Each participant underwent seven weeks of physical conditioning so that the steep climbs in the park would not be exhausting. Each person completed a two-hour course on how to avoid hypothermia, a potentially fatal condition brought on by getting wet without a chance to dry off. Wet clothing and wet skin can rapidly lower the body temperature to the point that death occurs, and hypothermia can set in at temperatures as high as 50 degrees Fahrenheit. In addition, each participant was to be properly equipped with a waterproof/windproof coat, good boots, and a sleeping bag, and each group carried enough food for ten days along with stoves and fuel. These careful preparations and a cautious attitude would save many lives in the spring of 1993.

A happy, excited group of students and faculty boarded buses in Detroit on March 6, 1993, for the trip to the Smoky Mountains. As the group traveled south, it seemed they were running into the very arms of spring. After the harsh Michigan winter, the temperatures in Tennessee seemed almost balmy. Even when the group arrived in the mountains and checked in with rangers on the North Carolina side of the park, the cool evenings did not seem much of a challenge.

Park officials, however, were concerned about the long-range forecast. Although predicting the weather a week in advance cannot be done with a great deal of accuracy, there were warnings about the possibility of a storm. The rangers knew the heaviest snow often comes to the park in the spring, so they advised the Cranbrook group to keep an eye on the weather and to carry out as much of their program as possible at lower elevations.

As the small groups of students and faculty entered the woods, they saw signs of the coming spring. Leaf buds were swollen, the ferns were poking "fiddleheads" up through the detritus of leaves, birdsong filled the air, and the sun felt warm on the students' shoulders.

The first days of the trip went as planned. Each group camped at a separate backcountry site and carried out their planned activities, working on developing outdoor and camping skills, enjoying nature, and bonding as a group. As the days passed and the weather seemed good, some of the groups moved higher up the mountains.

On Friday night, March 12, 1993, the Cranbrook School campers were spread over a wide area of the park, just as they had planned. They were approaching the end of their stay with only a few days left. That night, as the groups slept, the Blizzard of '93 struck. This massive storm brought bad weather from Key West to Nova Scotia, causing more than eight hundred million dollars in damages and taking the lives of 270 people. During the night of March 12/13 the barometer fell to 29.24 inches and the temperature sank to 13 degrees Fahrenheit.

The dramatic change in their conditions startled some of the students. One of them later said the scariest time of all was waking up to find three feet of snow on her tarpaulin shelter. Some of the groups recognized the futility of attempting to move and simply sat down to wait for a thaw. These groups were wise, but boredom made waiting difficult, and the uncertainty of their situation gnawed at their confidence.

Other groups began to move down the slopes of the mountains and immediately experienced difficulty. Any movement in the deep snow was difficult. Obstacles were hidden by the white blanket until hikers stumbled over them, and stream crossings often meant wet feet as stepping stones and foot logs were coated with ice. Such conditions also made it difficult to cook. Soon those groups trying to hike were tired and some signs of hypothermia and frostbite were becoming apparent.

Back in Detroit there was growing anxiety among the parents and relatives of the campers. The students stranded in the mountains had not carried walkie-talkies because the rugged terrain makes communication with such devices difficult and often impossible.

One group of students, accompanied by Marcy Paisley and Mark Penske, seemed to be at the limits of its physical ability. Several of the students felt they could go no farther, so a camp was made for the night. After all the students were settled in, Marcy and Mark set out to find help. They struggled through the woods for three miles and had gotten wet to the waist when they smelled smoke. Soon they were at the camp of some fishermen who dried them out, fed them, and told them that hundreds of National Guardsmen and park rangers were looking for the Cranbrook School groups.

The park authorities had reacted swiftly when the storm struck. As soon as the heavy snowfall lifted on Saturday, rangers began to follow the trails, some on foot and some on ATVs, looking for stranded hikers. The Tennessee and North Carolina National Guard were contacted for help. When the wind subsided enough to allow flight, army helicopters entered the search, some of the helicopters being provided by the 101st Airborne Division from Fort Campbell, Kentucky. On Monday hikers began to be brought out of the mountains. Helicopters spotted those needing help and rangers assisted by volunteer rescue units used ATVs to bring them out or helped the stranded hikers walk out. By Tuesday only twenty-four of the Cranbrook School group were unaccounted for. One group never even knew anyone was in trouble. This group completed its scheduled hiking, finished its programs, and walked out of the woods precisely at the time and place where they were expected. Still, there was great anxiety over the twenty-four who remained missing. At 1:30 p.m. on Tuesday, March 16, Chief Warrant Officer Glen Klutzz was flying his National Guard helicopter over one of the trails looking for the still-missing group of students. Klutzz popped over a ridge in the Hazel Creek area of the park, near Fontana Lake, and the remaining students were standing on the trail below, waving at him.

Some of the students had a rougher time than others. Danielle Swank recalled that the snow had begun suddenly and started to accumulate quickly. The students in her group set up their plastic tarpaulin shelters, but many of them collapsed during the night because of the weight of snow. With the snow continuing on Saturday morning, her group decided to head down the mountain, hoping to find less snow and better walking conditions. Danielle suffered from asthma and had had to ask another student to carry her pack on one occasion so, as the group moved down the mountain through the deep snow, she fell to the back of the line, walking slowly, hoping to avoid another asthma attack.

Slowly the rest of the group drew ahead but James Woodruff, a faculty member at the school, stayed with Danielle. By Saturday afternoon they had lost the tracks of the rest of the group because the trail the leading group broke was quickly covered by blowing snow. As darkness fell the two pitched their tarpaulin shelter, ate some food, and tried to keep warm. Danielle was unable to get one of her boots off and James could remove neither of his. The next morning Danielle could not replace the boot she had removed and James made the decision to go looking for help, leaving her his sleeping bag and most of their food.

All day Sunday Danielle hoped to hear the sound of help coming toward her, but she heard only the sounds of the winter forest. Woodruff never returned and, as night fell again, she was alone and worried. By Monday morning she was thirsty and even more worried. Then, about 3:00 p.m. she heard the sound of a helicopter and soon it was hovering over her location. In a few minutes she had a rescuer beside her and then was on her way to a hospital. James Woodruff was found, unconscious, about a half-mile from the campsite where he had left Danielle. Of the 116 students and faculty from Cranbrook School, these were the only two to require hospitalization.

This group of students had faced trying moments and had stiff physical challenges to meet, but good planning and careful preparation before setting out, along with a cautious approach to the mountains, brought out alive all those who went in together.

Of course, the Cranbrook School students were not the only hikers trapped by the storm. The Park Service brought out many others who found themselves needing help. Back-country rangers were brought in from all over the nation to help with the rescues. When the efforts and results of the rangers were evaluated, the Great Smoky Mountains National Park received a Department of the Interior Unit award with 167 park employees named for their efforts.

CHAPTER 13

Fatal Bear Attack

ONE OF THE GREAT ATTRACTIONS IN THE GREAT SMOKY Mountains are black bears that inhabit the park and can often be spotted from the road while driving along quiet stretches, especially in Cades Cove where there is open pasture land and the views are more extensive. Depending on the food supply and weather conditions during the previous winter, the park may be home to as many as eighteen hundred bears at any one time. Most visitors are quite excited by the prospect of seeing a bear in the wild, but most want that experience to occur at a distance. Perhaps the greatest fear expressed by inexperienced hikers is that of encountering a bear while on the trail. Experienced hikers know this is a rare occurrence and that the best way to avoid an unexpected encounter is to make a reasonable amount of noise while walking along. Almost always, black bears are anxious to avoid human contact and will move away from the sound of people. The North American Bear Center reports that between 1900 and 2007 sixty people were killed by black bear attacks in all of North America. Forty-five of these attacks took place in Canada and Alaska.

The black bears of the Great Smoky Mountains are of medium size with adults ranging in weight from 125 to 250 pounds, although both males and females put on weight as winter approaches. There are many sub-species of black bears, so those in other parts of the country may be somewhat different from those in the Smoky Mountains. In the wild a healthy black bear has a life expectancy of eighteen to twenty-three years. The Smoky Mountains black bears are not true hibernators, and a few may be seen roaming the woods if the winter is mild.

However, bears can become accustomed to being around people and lose their fear of human contact. This often happens when bears feed on garbage left at picnic grounds and begin to associate people with free food. Black bears, along with other wildlife, become "food conditioned" when people throw food to them in an attempt to coax the animal closer for a photo or when they become accustomed to eating garbage. Eating garbage may mean the bear swallows potato chip bags or fried chicken containers because they smell and taste salty or greasy, seriously injuring the health of the animal.

Consuming food meant for humans is bad for the bears because their health can be affected negatively, they stay in areas where there is more vehicle traffic and are more likely to be hit by a car, or because they injure a park visitor and the Park Service has to kill the animal. Bears are wild animals that must be treated with respect and should never be approached. For the same reason, hikers who plan to spend the night at backcountry campsites are required to suspend packs and food supplies from a line strung between two trees so as to frustrate the attempt of bears to get at their food. These precautions usually protect hikers and backpackers from unwanted encounters with bears. Whether seen from the window of an automobile or glimpsed through the woods while on a trail, park regulations require visitors to stay fifty yards away from animals. If the animal changes their behavior as you approach, you are too close!

Such precautions usually protect a hiker, but not always! In the entire history of the Great Smoky Mountains National Park, stretching back more than eighty years, there has been only one fatal attack by a bear on a hiker.

Glenda Ann Bradley lived in Cosby, Tennessee, on the eastern edge of the park. She was an experienced hiker, taught at a local elementary school, and, at age fifty, was very fit. On Sunday, May 21, 2000, a fine spring day, she accompanied Ralph Hill, a neighbor and her former husband, on a trip to the Elkmont area of the park. Ralph planned to fish in the Goshen Prong of the Little River while Glenda hiked. They parked at the Little River Trail trailhead near the Elkmont Campground about noon and strolled along the flat, easy trail that once was the bed of a logging railroad. After about two miles the trail narrowed as they reached the vicinity of the junction of Goshen Prong with Little River. Ralph went along the banks of the stream, looking for a likely pool in which to cast his fly, and Glenda wandered along the nearby trail.

After fishing a short while Ralph went to look for his companion and, much to his surprise, found her daypack. Looking carefully into the surrounding foliage, he was horrified to see Glenda's body with two bears standing over it, a female of medium size and a yearling female cub. When Ralph attempted to scare the bears away, the larger of the two showed aggressive behavior toward him so he went to get help.

Ralph shared the news of the tragedy with others who came along the trail, and one of these hikers made a quick run to the ranger station at Elkmont to report the incident. The report was received at 5:00 p.m., and a ranger was on the scene by 6:00 with two additional rangers arriving in a few minutes. Since the bears were still near the body, the rangers shot both animals with their service weapons.

The necropsy report on the two bears showed that the adult bear was a 112-pound female and the smaller cub was a female weighing forty pounds. Both animals had fed on the body of the deceased hiker. The larger of the pair had been tagged in 1998 by wildlife biologists from the University of Tennessee for research purposes, and there was no report of previous aggressive behavior toward humans.

An autopsy concluded that Glenda Bradley died from loss of blood caused by the injuries inflicted by the bears. Her daypack, which contained food, had not been disturbed and there was no evidence that she had in any way provoked the fatal attack. Glenda had simply encountered an animal that is wild and unpredictable and should always be treated with caution and respect.

Even if the larger area surrounding the park is considered, bear attacks are rare. Stretching south and southwest of the Great Smoky Mountains National Park is a section of the

Cherokee National Forest, while another section of the Forest lies east and north of the park. The Cherokee National Forest contains over 655,000 acres and, with the Great Smoky Mountains, provides a large habitat for bears, being home to an estimated fifteen hundred of the animals. In 2006 a fatal bear attack took place in the Cherokee National Forest several miles southeast of the park.

Susan Paul Cenkus had grown up near the Cherokee National Forest and the Great Smoky Mountains. As a child she often visited Benton Falls, one of the favorite spots for those who know the Forest. The approach to the falls is along a Forest Service road that leads seven miles from US 64 to McKamy Lake and the Chilhowee Day Use Area. From the swimming area on McKamy Lake, an easy one and one-half mile trail leads to Benton Falls. The cascade is sixty-five feet high and widens toward the bottom of its descent, tumbling into a pool that is deep enough for swimming and devoid of dangerous currents unless the water is very high.

Following her marriage Susan moved to Ohio, but one of her sons returned to the area where she was born to enter college. The younger children in the family, including her daughter Elora Petrasek, a child of her first marriage, often heard her mother talk about the beauty of the Cherokee Forest and of Benton Falls. They frequently expressed a wish to visit the places their mother described.

In April 2006, the family decided to pay a visit to their son for a special event at his college in Tennessee. While there, they decided to make a family outing to Benton Falls. When they arrived at the falls, they found several other family groups enjoying playing in the water and soaking up the sun and scenery of the area. As the afternoon began to wane, one of the groups left the falls, only to return in a short time reporting that they had seen a bear. No sooner had this report been given than the bear burst out of the brush and approached the group. All the adults shouted and tried to frighten the animal away, but the bear seized Susan's son, Luke, only two years old, by the head. Susan reacted as any mother would and attacked the bear with only her hands. The bear responded by dropping Luke and seizing Susan, dragging her into the surrounding woods. Chaos followed with some people running toward the parking area and others trying to chase away the bear. In the confusion Susan's daughter, Elora, disappeared.

Some of those who had run for their cars returned with reinforcements and found that those who had stayed behind had been successful in rescuing Susan from her attacker. Others had made a cellphone call to the local emergency services so an ambulance and law enforcement officers were soon on the scene. Susan, badly mauled, was placed in an ambulance and was soon on her way to a major hospital in Chattanooga, Tennessee. Then someone noticed that Elora was missing.

Members of the local rescue team had arrived to assist by this time, and some of them volunteered to mount a search for the missing girl. As the searchers reached the area near the falls, one of them spotted a bear hovering over Elora's body. Gunfire drove the bear away, and the rescuers used their shirts to cover the body until paramedics could arrive.

Susan was put into a drug-induced coma for nine days and underwent several surgeries to repair the wounds inflicted by the bear. Her son, Luke, recovered quickly and was released from the hospital within a week. He did not seem to have any psychological trauma from the attack. Two bears were trapped near Benton Falls, and DNA tests showed one of them to have been the attacker. This animal was killed. Several months later the surviving family returned to Benton Falls to add memories of good times to the lasting thoughts of the tragedy. The death of Elora Petrasek is only the second fatality caused by a bear attack recorded in Tennessee history.

All bear attacks are frightening, but not all are fatal. On August 12, 2008, a black bear yearling attacked Evan Pala, eight years old, while he was playing in a stream near the start of the Rainbow Falls Trail on the Roaring Fork Motor Nature Trail, one of the most visited locations in the Great Smoky Mountains National Park. While Evan was playing the small bear approached and attacked the boy. John Pala, Evan's father, shouted, threw sticks and rocks and drove the bear away, only to see it return for a second attack. Again John was successful in defending his son. Park Service employees responded to the report of the incident, and Evan and John were taken to a hospital in Sevierville. They were treated for puncture wounds before being released a few hours later.

Rangers searched the area where the attack took place and encountered a young male black bear that approached them in an aggressive manner. When they were unable to chase the animal away, it was shot. A child's shoe and cap were found in the vicinity. In this case the Palas got a bad scare but escaped mortal injuries.

On May 17, 2010, Sean Konover was hiking the Laurel Falls Trail, a route so popular that it is paved and is often used by parents of young children who push their infants in strollers. Suddenly a small black bear came out of the bushes alongside the trail, and people quickly gathered for a photo opportunity. The small bear looked cute but, as the crowd grew, it became nervous, and when Sean came really near for a close-up shot the cub nipped him on the foot. The cub ran away as the crowd melted back, and an examination showed that the bite was so minor that no medical attention was needed. This was a matter of bad judgment and good luck.

Gabriel Alexander exercised good judgment and had bad luck. Greg Alexander and his sixteen-year-old son, Gabriel, drove from Athens, Ohio, with the intent of taking a fifty-mile hike, lasting several days, in the Great Smoky Mountains. Both father and son were physically fit; Gabriel was a member of his high school track team, and they were prepared for the backpacking hike. Their planned route took them into the south and southwest sections of the park that border on Lake Fontana, an area less visited by backpackers. The first days of their trip went as planned, and they had covered about forty miles of their route when they made camp in the backcountry at Campsite #84 near Hazel Creek. There the pair slung the hammocks they preferred for sleeping, cooked their supper, and slung their packs and food supplies to a "bear cable" mounted between two trees. They cleaned up their campsite so there were no food scraps or trash in the area, and went to bed. Long days on the trail make for early nights. So far, the pair had done everything one is supposed to do to be a good, safe backpacker.

It was 10:30 p.m. and Gabriel was fast asleep when he was shocked awake by a searing pain in his head and scalp—a bear had seized him by the head and was dragging him from his hammock!

He could not reach the bear, but his cries woke his father, Greg, who attacked the bear, kicking it with his bare feet. That had no effect, so Greg jumped on the back of the bear and pummeled it with his fists. At last the animal dropped Gabriel and ran off into the darkness, although it could still be heard circling the pair.

It was impossible to see the extent of Gabriel's injuries by the light available to Greg, but it was clear help had to be found as soon as possible. Wrapping his son's head in a shirt, Greg helped Gabriel begin the slow and painful hike to Lake Fontana, some five miles away. Hiking at night is never easy, even with a good flashlight or headlamp, and this was an especially difficult trek since Gabriel needed support to make it through the sometimes uneven terrain. Just as it was getting light, the two reached the shore of the lake and, happily, soon found two men at Campsite #86 who had a boat with an outboard motor. These Good Samaritans gave the Alexanders a ride to the Cable Cove boat dock where first aid was administered and an ambulance was called.

Gabriel was taken to a hospital in Asheville, North Carolina, where he spent several days. There was no fracturing of his skull and the bites to his head did not involve his eyes, although some cosmetic surgery would later be required. From his hospital bed Gabriel portrayed the true spirit of an outdoorsman when he said he did not want the bear killed but he sure hoped it would not attack anyone else. The Park Service protocols for bear attacks, however, required that the animal be found and killed and this was done. Gabriel added that he knew events such as he had experienced were rare, and he did not think his encounter with a bear should make anyone afraid to enjoy the mountains.

People who are not acquainted with wildlife often hold one of two contrasting views about bears. One view sees them as fearsome monsters, cold-blooded killers, who roam the wilderness ready to pounce on the unwary from behind every bush. There is a huge volume of tradition and literature that presents this view and, for those who accept it, the forest of the Great Smoky Mountains is a foreboding place that is safe only when one is ensconced behind the windows of an automobile. The second contingent believes all bears are like Yogi at Jellystone Park, fun-loving, rollicking furry friends ready to welcome human advances. Those who hold this view run toward bears when they are sighted alongside roads, throw them apples and candy bars, and even try to pose for pictures with the animals. Those who accept this view can, and do, engage in foolish actions that can result in harm to themselves and to the bears.

Both these views are false. Bears are wild animals. They are unpredictable, although they usually try to avoid human contact unless conditioned to do otherwise. But they can hurt you; they can kill you. Wildlife should be enjoyed, but they should be treated with caution and with respect.

CHAPTER 14

Deadly Winds, Dangerous Waters, and Distracted Drivers

THE GREAT SMOKY MOUNTAINS NATIONAL PARK CONTAINS very few roads. The main thoroughfare is the Trans-Mountain Road, officially called US 441, which connects Gatlinburg, Tennessee, on the north side of the park, with Cherokee, North Carolina, on the south side. This road is closed to commercial traffic. At the Sugarlands Visitors Center, near Gatlinburg, the Little River Road goes west off the Trans-Mountain Road and leads to an intersection called the Wye where one fork of the road continues to Cades Cove and the other exits the park to go to Townsend, Tennessee. At Newfound Gap, on the Gatlinburg to Cherokee road, another road goes west to Clingmans Dome to provide access to an observation tower and trailheads. In addition to these, there are some roads that lead from the outside of the park to various attractions a few miles inside the park, but these are not through roads and end at a destination in the park. All park roads are closed to commercial traffic. None of the roads are constructed for high-speed travel; their purpose is to allow visitors to enjoy the mountain scenery and to reach destinations within the park. The roads are narrow, have hills and curves that limit the line of sight of drivers, and usually do not have guardrails. The speed limit on most park roads is 30 miles per hour or less.

Ten million visitors annually use this limited road net, most of them driving from one side of the park to the other and then visiting Clingmans Dome and Cades Cove. In short, a great deal of traffic uses only a few miles of roads within the park. Some drivers are distracted by the scenery and try to look at the view while driving, instead of taking advantage of the numerous pull-offs that provide parking for safe viewing; other drivers are impaired because they have consumed alcohol, and some just become careless. Driving while distracted or drunk is not a problem unique to the park, but it is the leading cause of death in the Great Smoky Mountains. Death caused by an automobile accident is tragic whenever and wherever it occurs, but it is especially poignant when it takes place in a beautiful setting while the victim is on vacation.

In August 1994 Patti Szuber, a nursing student from Berkley, Michigan, visited the Smoky Mountains with her friend, Todd Herbst. The trip was a welcome break from the rigors of her nursing studies and, in a phone call home soon after she arrived in the park, Patti told her mother she was having a wonderful time. This changed suddenly and tragically on the night of August 18 when she and Todd were driving in an unsafe manner on one of the park roads. Their car ran off the road, struck a rock bluff, careened back onto the road, and rolled over several times.

When law enforcement rangers and an ambulance arrived, they found Todd had only minor injuries, but Patti was seriously injured. They also found Todd had a blood alcohol level over the legal limit, meaning he was driving while drunk, and that he had a suspended driver's license.

Patti was airlifted to the University of Tennessee Medical Center in Knoxville, some forty miles away, but her prognosis was very poor. She was in extremely critical condition, and when her family arrived to be with her they were offered little hope. Within a few hours Patti was pronounced brain dead.

Patti had indicated much earlier that she wanted to donate her viable organs in case of her death, and the family proceeded to honor her wish. But there was an unusual twist to their decision.

Chester Szuber, Patti's father, suffered from life-threatening irregularities of his heartbeat, and over the past twenty years he had undergone three open-heart surgeries and two angioplasties. Chester was on the waiting list for a heart transplant, and tests showed that Patti was a compatible donor.

Now the family faced another dilemma. The heart transplant would be a risky operation and Chester might not survive, but without a transplant his life expectancy was limited. After deliberation Chester announced that it "would be a joy to have Patti's heart." A team of surgeons went to work immediately, a plane was standing by when the procedure in Knoxville was completed, and just under six hours after

Patti's heart had stopped beating in her body it was beating inside the body of her father. The sadness of the loss of a daughter was mixed with the joy of the chance at new life offered a father.

◄══►

On March 26, 2005, Jonathan Hall and Steven Williams made the worst mistake of their young lives. Jonathan was nineteen years old and lived in Lebanon, Tennessee; Steve was twenty-one and was from Murfreesboro, Tennessee. Jonathan owned a 1991 Honda Accord and Steve drove a 1996 Nissan 240 SX. Like many young men they were proud of their cars and liked to demonstrate that they had the better vehicle when any comparison was being made. Somehow this pride in their vehicles led to tragedy.

How and why the decision was made is now irrelevant, but Jonathan and Steve decided to use US 441, inside the Great Smoky Mountains National Park, as a drag strip. Speeding down the curvy road, side-by-side, they rounded a bend to see a 1997 Chrysler in front of them. The Chrysler swerved but Jonathan Hall hit it directly in the side. Steven Williams managed to swerve around the crash and kept going. In the car were George and Myra Nelson; Audrey Fentress, Myra's mother; and Anthony and Betty Dietz. The occupants of the Chrysler ranged in age from sixty-four to eighty-four.

All the passengers in the Chrysler were killed, though Hall survived. This is the most deadly auto accident ever to take place in the park. Hall was taken to a hospital in Knoxville but was released pending the completion of an investigation. Because the fatal accident had taken place in a national park, federal law enforcement authorities conducted the investigation.

In January 2006, Jonathan Hall and Steven Williams were arrested on a federal warrant and charged with five counts of second-degree murder. The indictment against them said "each aided and abetted and induced the other, with malice aforethought, whereas they did unlawfully kill five human beings." The indictment continued: "Both were driving in a reckless manner and with extreme disregard for human life, in that they were operating their motor vehicles at an extremely high rate of speed and were drag racing." The two men struck a plea deal to have the charges against them reduced to one count of second-degree murder and were duly sentenced. Jonathan Hall received twenty-one years and ten months in prison and Steven Williams was sentenced to eight and a half years.

The park superintendent at the time, Dale Ditmanson, noted that "speeding is a very serious problem on US 441 and drag racing, in particular, creates a very hazardous environment, endangering the lives of not only those breaking the law but also innocent motorists such as in this case. Motor vehicle accidents are by far the largest source of fatalities in the park."

Not only do automobile crashes endanger visitors, they put at risk park rangers and the volunteers who assist them. On Sunday, December 11, 2011, Ranger Bradley Griest responded to a call that a car had run off the Little River

Road and that the driver was trapped in the partially sub-merged vehicle. On arrival at the scene Griest saw that a pickup truck was at the bottom of a twenty-foot embank-ment and some three feet out into the stream. Climbing down the embankment the ranger jumped onto the car and struggled to open the door, but the force of the fast-moving current was more than he could overcome. As Griest tried to find a way to get the trapped driver out of the crushed cab of the car and out of the 45-degree water, Christopher Scarbrough came on the scene. Scarbrough was a member of the Townsend Volunteer Fire Department and, seeing the ranger in need of assistance, put on a life jacket and helmet, scrambled down the embankment, jumped over the three-foot gap, and called for a winch cable to be lowered. Work-ing in the dark and splashed by the frigid water, Griest and Scarbrough attached the cable to the door of the truck and the winch operator pulled it open far enough for the driver to be extracted. The driver was taken to the hospital, suffer-ing from the onset of hypothermia as well as from injuries from the crash, but he later made a full recovery.

It was the opinion of park officials that the ranger and volunteer fireman saved a life by risking their own. For their bravery Ranger Bradley Griest received the Valor Award from the National Park Service and Christopher Scarbrough received the Citizens Award.

~

Frank Lohmann was not lucky enough to be rescued, although people tried to save him. On December 20, 2013, Lohm-ann of nearby Maryville, Tennessee, was driving in the park not far from where Griest and Scarbrough had performed their heroic rescue. Just before 3:00 p.m. his automobile was struck by one driven by Brett Adams, a resident of Louisville, Kentucky. Lohmann's car ran off the road and flipped upside down in the frigid waters of Little River. Drivers who came along a few minutes later, park rangers, and emergency crews from Townsend all tried to get the elderly driver from his car, but the rescue was slow and difficult. The eighty-three-year-old was pronounced dead at the scene. Adams was cited for unsafe operation of a motor vehicle and driving without insurance.

Ironically, the man who did more than any single individual to bring about the creation of the Great Smoky Mountains National Park, Horace Kephart, was killed in a traffic accident in 1931, before the park became a reality. Traffic accidents are in the news every day in large cities, but death by auto crash seems cruel in the midst of such natural beauty as is found in the Great Smoky Mountains National Park.

On the southwest side of the Smoky Mountains park lies US 129, not a road known to most people, but to motorcycle riders and sportscar buffs an eleven-mile stretch of this road is famous and is known as "The Tail of the Dragon." This stretch is bordered by the national park on one side and by the Cherokee National Forest on the other, so there are no intersecting roads or driveways. Both North Carolina and Tennessee ban trucks over thirty feet in length from this road, so there are no "big-rig" trucks for riders to worry about. There are 318 curves in this eleven-mile stretch of highway, with some of the curves having names such as Copperhead Corner, Hog Pen Bend, Wheelie Hell, Gravity Cavity, and Brake or Bust. The posted speed limit on the Tail is 30 miles per hour, but the drive is rated as one of the "ten best" motorcycle and sportscar drives in the nation. People come from all over the world to ride The Tail of the Dragon. On their way to, or from, the Tail, many motorcycle riders visit the Great Smoky Mountains National Park.

With some drivers distracted from the road by watching the scenery, with narrow roads where it is easy to drift over the center line, and with some drivers going faster than the posted limit, it is clear that motorcyclists are at risk. In 2004 there were six traffic fatalities in the park, and four of them involved people riding motorcycles. Two fatal examples that occurred only a few days apart a few years later illustrate this point.

Charles and Diane Bolt, both in their mid-fifties, loved riding motorcycles, and in August 2009, they decided to ride from their home in Belton, South Carolina, to the nearby Great Smoky Mountains. On this trip Diane would ride pillion behind her husband. Both were experienced riders who had traveled by motorcycle for many years, and they were enjoying the scenery and fresh air when they crossed the Tennessee–North Carolina state line at Newfound Gap just about 11:30 a.m. Just a couple of miles farther down the Tennessee side of the mountains, a sport utility vehicle going up the mountain side-swiped another car, crossed into the downhill lane, and hit the Bolts head on. The SUV ran into a ditch and overturned, though none of the occupants were seriously injured. The Bolts were killed instantly.

Less than a month later, on September 2, 2009, Albert Green, sixty-nine years old, from Waukesha, Wisconsin, lost control of his machine and ran off the road on the Tail. He became the fourth fatality on that road for the year.

Sadly, deaths involving motorcycle riders continue to occur. On April 18, 2015, Serbey Chenkov of Jacksonville, Florida, was killed in a motorcycle crash two miles west of the Elkmont Campground road while riding on the Little River Road.

Water sports are not recommended in the Great Smoky Mountains National Park, although on any day during hot weather visitors can be seen wading in the shallows or floating on tubes where the water is deeper. Few stretches of the rivers within the park are both free of obstructions and deep enough to allow the use of kayaks, although some can be seen, especially following rains when the water level is high. This is also the most dangerous time to be on these mountain rivers, and deaths do occur on the waters. On June 15, 2015, there was a thunderstorm in the Ramsay Cascade area of the park, although the sun continued to shine and not a drop of water fell in the Greenbrier section, only five miles away. Shortly after the storm dumped its load of water near Mount Guyot, a wall of water six feet in height came rushing down the Middle Prong of the Little Pigeon River. The water level in the river doubled in depth, and the stream tripled in width in less than ten minutes. A rain miles away can suddenly change the character of a stream in the Smoky Mountains.

Climbing on and swimming under waterfalls are the most dangerous water activities in the park. There are many hazards underneath the surface of pools at the foot of waterfalls, and the rocks at the sides of the falls are covered with slick algae and moss. It is easy to slip and fall onto rocks below or to fall into the water and be trapped by the current or by obstructions in the pool. The falls with the most volume of water going over it of any in the park is Abrams Falls. This is also the most dangerous of the falls.

The trail to Abrams Falls is reached by turning off the Cades Cove loop road for a short drive to a parking area. From the parking lot a short hike of just over two and a half miles brings the hiker to Abrams Falls. The falls is only twenty feet in height, but a very large volume of water rushes over it, forming a deep and sparkling pool at the foot of the drop. Despite the picturesque and inviting nature of the pool, swimming in it is very dangerous because of strong currents and the presence of an undertow. Since 1971 there have been twenty-nine deaths in water-related accidents at Abrams Falls.

Vivek Kumaralingham, twenty-six years old, was a resident of Manchester, Connecticut, where he was employed by a technology company. With two companions he came to visit the Great Smoky Mountains National Park in July 2006. On July 2 the trio hiked the trail to Abrams Falls and decided to swim in the pool beneath the falls. Vivek was a good swimmer, and he was enjoying the water when he decided to swim under water toward the base of the falls. Apparently, he was caught by the undertow beneath the falls and never surfaced. Park rangers and rescue divers used pack mules to haul diving equipment to the Falls, and they recovered the body the following day.

Just two years earlier a thirteen-year-old boy from Knoxville had drowned at the same spot. Christopher Drinkard was a student at Vine Middle School and had spent the entire school year enrolled in the Smoky Mountains Science Class, an experience that culminated in a field trip to the area they had studied all year. Forty-one students and four adult chaperones traveled by school bus to Abrams Falls Trail on a late April day, then the group hiked to the falls. Christopher was wearing his regular clothes, jeans and a shirt, when he seems to have fallen into the water. Two adults rushed to help get him back to safety, but they could not reach him and he disappeared beneath the surface of the pool. A message was sent to park officials and the remainder of the students returned to their bus. Park rangers trained in handling critical incident stress met the bus and talked to the group before they returned home.

Just before 6:00 p.m. divers found the body of the boy in thirty feet of water, trapped by the swift current against a rock. Visibility at that depth was less than one foot. Christopher was an outstanding student, had an excellent character, and followed the rules his teachers set. He was the victim of an unfortunate accident.

The quiet of Cades Cove was shattered on Sunday, May 24, 2009, as an ambulance and Park Service vehicles raced along the narrow loop road to the trailhead for Abrams Falls. There had been a great deal of rain over the weekend, and the water in Abrams Creek was quite high. A group of foreign nationals, students at Penn State University, had come to visit the park on an informal trip. While visiting the falls Nublan Zaki Norhadi fell into the water, probably because the rocks around the falls were slick and wet. Nublan was not a strong swimmer and went beneath the surface almost immediately. The incident was reported to park officials about 7:00 p.m., but darkness prevented the recovery of the body until the next day.

———

Another place of great beauty and of great danger is the bend in Little River located twelve miles west of the Sugarlands Visitors Center on the Little River Road. This location is called "The Sinks" because the water "sinks" into a pool before boiling up again. Here the Little River makes an "s" turn while the river is narrowed by rock formations. The entire flow of the river is forced over cascades and a low waterfall, while the speed of the current increases rapidly because of the narrowing of the channel. Low bluffs overlook the pool created by the river as it makes the final part of its turn. The rapid current and the swift plunge attract kayakers, and the bluffs tempt people to jump into the pool even though signs are posted prominently warning of hidden obstructions and undertows.

On June 5, 2007, park rangers and rescue personnel were called to The Sinks to search for the body of Joshua Robertson, age twenty-four, who lived in Maryville, Tennessee. Joshua had decided to scoot down the rocks to water level to take pictures of the rushing water. When he tried to stand up, he lost his footing on the slick rocks and fell into the water. Two of his friends, as well as several other people, witnessed the accident, but Joshua never resurfaced so no help could be offered. Some of the witnesses drove into Townsend, where cellphone service was available. Park rangers and the local rescue squad brought in scuba diving equipment, and the body of the young man was found pinned against rocks deep under the surface several hours after the fall took place.

Amber Rose Mirisola, age seventeen, from Mount Dore, Florida, stopped with her family at The Sinks on July 30, 2011. Like so many others, she was fascinated at the breathtaking beauty of the spot and decided to get closer for a better look. She was standing at the top of the falls when she slipped on the mossy rocks and fell fifteen feet before hitting the water below. The undertow trapped her between two rocks and kept her deep under water. Visitors who were at the scene formed a human chain and tried to reach the girl, but the current was too strong for them to be successful. Rescue teams had to use a rope and pulley system to pull her body free.

On the same day, a few miles west of The Sinks, at the Wye in the Little River Road near Townsend, Dick Chijioke, thirty-four, from Plano, Texas, was floating on a tube at an area where the Little River is about to leave the park. At the Wye the river becomes straighter, wider, and deeper as it reaches the head of a valley. This is a popular spot for swimming, wading, and tubing. In Townsend several companies rent tubes, and on hot days this area of the river hosts scores of people enjoying the water. Chijioke was tubing with his family when he slipped out of his tube in twelve feet of water and did not resurface. Help was summoned from Townsend, and the local rescue team reported the incident to the park officials. The call for help was received at 11:22 a.m., and the body was recovered just over an hour later.

The Sinks claimed another victim on March 12, 2013. Stewart Senior, age sixty-five, of Northbridge, Ontario, was visiting the park with a group of canoe and kayak enthusiasts. In attempting to run the rapids at The Sinks, his boat overturned and Stewart became trapped. It took his friends and park rangers thirty minutes to recover his body.

~

The West Prong of the Little Pigeon River flows alongside the Trans-Mountain Road, though often out of sight of the highway, in the vicinity of the Sugarlands Visitors Center. The Road Prong of the river branches off from the West Prong and leads up the mountains through the Chimney Tops Picnic Area. Normally the Road Prong is too shallow for kayaks, but on August 27, 2008, there had been so much rain that this section of the Pigeon River could be navigated in kayaks. Isaac Ludwig, Jared Seiler, and James Donahue, all experienced kayakers, decided to take advantage of these conditions to run the Road Prong in their craft. Soon after entering the stream, Jared and James decided that the water was too high and too swift, so they ran their kayaks ashore and took them out of the water. Isaac continued on, but he did not reach the agreed rendezvous point. A search was initiated, and two days later his body was found when the water level dropped. Isaac was experienced in kayaking, worked for a rafting company on one of the rivers outside the park, and was wearing a life vest and a helmet.

The weekend of July 4, 2015, was marked by heavy thunderstorms in the Great Smoky Mountains National Park, but the holiday weekend still brought a throng of visitors. Among them was Kenneth Worthington, fifty-three years old, who came to the Greenbrier section of the park with some friends for the purpose of kayaking on the Middle Prong of the Little Pigeon River. Although the river was high, the group went ahead with their plans only to see the kayak with Worthington aboard capsize. Kenneth floated to the edge of the stream, and his friends pulled him out. CPR was performed but the unfortunate man was pronounced dead at a local hospital.

The streams in the Great Smoky Mountains are indeed beautiful and they should be enjoyed, but they should be treated with caution and respect. It is too often the case that a visitor drowns in beauty.

Deadly winds swept the park on July 5, 2012. Severe thunderstorms hit the high peaks of the mountains, causing flash floods, and a tornado ranked as an EF-4 with winds up to 165 miles per hour cut a swath one mile wide and twenty miles in length, knocking down forty-five hundred trees. These storms closed thirty-five miles of trails and caused two deaths.

The first area of the park to feel the wrath of the storm was Cades Cove. As the storm roared over the valley and trees began to topple, closing the road, one park visitor suffered a heart attack, a second had a back injury when he was struck by a falling tree, and a third received facial cuts when a tree shattered the windshield on his car. But the worst accident came on the road leading from the Wye to Cades Cove. Ralph Frazier, fifty, of Buford, Georgia, had been visiting the park and was riding his motorcycle toward Townsend when the storm unleashed its fury. Of course, braving the weather is part of what has to be done when riding a motorcycle, so Ralph pushed on. Without warning a large limb crashed down from a tree just as he was passing under it and he was killed instantly. So many trees were down that it took emergency crews six hours to clear a path for emergency vehicles to reach Cades Cove, Ralph Frazier, and the injured park visitors there.

At the Abrams Creek campground and picnic area, there was no warning of the approaching storm. This area is located on the northwest side of the park and is reached by a road leading from the Chilhowee community and the Foothills Parkway. It is off the main roads used by most park visitors, but it is popular with local residents. The winds suddenly picked up and rain began to fall. Several people were swimming and splashing in a creek there when a tree suddenly fell right into the midst of the group. Visitors rushed to assist those hit by the tree, but two needed immediate attention. A seven-year-old girl was trapped under water by the tree, and there was a desperate scramble to get her free of the entangling branches. CPR was administered by a volunteer, who then used a satellite phone to contact the local emergency services offices, and the child was revived. Her father, who had been standing beside her when the tree fell, suffered broken ribs, a collapsed lung, and back injuries. Not so lucky was Rachel Burkhart. She was killed when the tree fell into the group of swimmers.

Given the number of visitors in the park at the time of the storm, and given the heavily wooded terrain of the park, the loss of life from this storm was amazingly small. While some lives are lost to hypothermia, other weather-related deaths in the Great Smoky Mountains are rare.

Dangerous winds, deadly waters, and distracted drivers are real hazards. Park visitors should not fear these dangers, but they should take appropriate precautions. If you are on the trail when an especially high wind arises, you should look for shelter beside a large rock or beside a fallen log. These will help protect you from falling trees. Heed the posted warnings about the dangers of climbing on waterfalls or on rocks in streams. Above all, pay attention to weather forecasts and keep an eye on the sky yourself. A little caution will provide a lot of protection and will make your visit to the Great Smoky Mountains National Park more enjoyable.

Index

About the Author

Michael R. Bradley taught US history at Motlow College in Lynchburg, Tennessee, from 1970 to 2006. He has hiked and camped in the Great Smoky Mountains National Park for more than forty-five years and continues to do so with his wife and grandchildren. He is the author of *It Happened In the Revolutionary War*, *It Happened In the Civil War*, *Myths and Mysteries of the Civil War*, and *It Happened In the Great Smokies*.